Worth Works

An Assertion About Life and God

Michael M. Kerns

ISBN-13: 978-1494946579
ISBN-10: 1494946572

©2014 Michael Kerns
First Edition 2014 CreateSpace

All Rights Reserved. No part of this book may be reproduced in part or in whole, by any means, except for brief quotations embodied in articles and reviews, without the express written consent of the publisher.

Unless otherwise indicated, all Scripture quotations are taken from the *King James Version* or from the author's own translation.

To Rusty Stambaugh
who lived too short a life but lived it well enough to let others know that "worth works" and reminded me to continue to persevere in spite of pain or disappointment.

Acknowledgments

To Stacy Tyson who volunteered for the unheralded task of putting the book into a format that would invite others to read and to give them the opportunity to understand it.

To Todd Jones who diligently read the earlier versions of this book, found numerous errors and made comments that contributed to a stronger presentation.

To David DeWitt who modeled for me the value of working diligently at understanding hard concepts and communicating them simply and for giving me the support and opportunities to to present them creatively to others.

To John Lipscomb who at regular and long breakfast times reminded me that the strong meat of truth never goes out of style and neither does grace run low.

To the Board of The Barnabas Associates—Napoleon Cassibry, Russell Clack, Michael Honan, John May, Michael McManus and Lawrence Miller—who have supported and accompanied me on this stewardship to present truth in clarity and in love.

To my son, Benjamin, who put in the time and the creativity to design the cover that I desired.

And, of course, to Joyce—wife, best friend and companion—who has acted as a patient sounding board and a constant cheerleader in listening to my constant barrage of ideas.

Contents

Acknowledgments 5

Worth Saying 11

INTRODUCTION

Worth Beginning 15

Worth Defining 17

Worth Continuing 21

PART ONE:
WORTH LOSING

1. The Pursuit of Possessions. 27

2. The Pursuit of Pleasure. 39

3. The Pursuit of Prestige 47

4. The Pursuit of People 59

WORTH THINKING

5. The Trouble with Truth 71

PART TWO:
WORTH PURSUING *A PROPOSAL*

6. The Undeniability of Death:
Who Can Escape Death? 87

7. Gaining Worth by Overcoming Death . . .103

8. The Necessity of God's Work of Worth
to Overcome Death. 117

9. The Incarnation of the Son of God 123
10. Reprisal: How Do We Survive Eternal Death? 137
11. How Will We Make A Decision? 145
12. How Do We Gain The Hope Of Worth? . . . 153

Summary of Part Two

Part Three: Worth Continuing

13. The Added Worth of Justification. 167
14. The Added Worth of Freedom 175
15. The Added Worth of Ambition 185
16. The Added Worth of Stewardship. 191
17. The Added Worth of Love 201
18. The Added Worth of Peace 205
19. The Added Worth of Forgiveness 221
20. The Added Worth of Change 235
21. The Added Worth of Suffering 249
22. The Added Worth of Graduation 265

Reprise

23. Your Worth Works 277

Worth Returning

Worth Saying

Authors write for a variety of reasons. A reader might be enlivened by a good novel, encouraged by a self-help book or further educated by a technical manual. When it comes to a book about what really matters in terms of the meaning of life, a writer runs the risk of sounding self-righteous or even worse of condemning others. I wish to do neither but I do understand that risk primarily with those whom I know and love.

Like the scientist whose conclusions that we have yet to see, I write so that you readers can have an open hearing about the following conclusions. I have written to encourage my friends and my family who seek and may already have a multiplied worth but have forgotten what they really have. I have also written to you whose pursuits come down to an illusory and fateful end because of a failed interpretation of life or, as we say, a false world-view.

You may not have truly considered the life of true worth and still live in a way that neither adds worth nor satisfies. To you I say, consider the thoughts of the following pages.

Michael Kerns
April 15, 2014
bulammk@yahoo.com

Introduction

Worth *Beginning*

"Man is but a reed, the most feeble thing in nature; but he is a thinking reed."

Blaise Pascal, philosopher and mathematician

Who I am matters; what I do matters. On February 12, 1968, the sanitation workers of Memphis, Tennessee staged a strike after the accidental death of two workers. Outsiders could characterize their walkout as unnecessary just for an almost inconsequential raise. Sanitation workers would argue it much differently. They had walked not just for a few cents more per hour for their dirty and backbreaking work of wheeling garbage and trash in a metal tub from people's backyards to an idling curbside truck. They had walked out to gain respect.

Who could foresee that some sixty-four days later when the strike concluded in a favorable agreement with the workers that this walkout would have a dramatic and lasting effect not just on the struggle for civil rights and labor in America but also on all Americans. Too many may forget the exact cause but they cannot forget the "I Have a Dream" speech and the death of Martin Luther King, Jr. who went to Memphis to support the workers. That strike also left remarkable and unforgettable photographs because of a timeless message. In a photograph, a lone black man in a business suit and hat walks on the sidewalk beside a

National Guard armored personnel carrier bedecked with armed and battle dressed soldiers. On the shoulders of the black protester rests a large two-sided sandwich board that simply described the heart of the walkout and depicts every person's struggle. The sandwich board read, "I am a man."

At a glance, the strike may have meant an opportunity for no more degradation by verbal abuse or better working conditions or more money. Men who did backbreaking and humiliating work to collect stinking garbage just wanted a union to argue their cause but it went deeper than that. These striking workers saw a denial of their raise as a denial of their dignity, a devaluing of their worth. Historians of different persuasions could look back and praise or denigrate the choices of the mayor or the workers but the idea on the placard of the strikers cannot be denied. It implied quite simply what we all want and need: worth.

Worth *Defining*

Whatever definition these men gave to worth, each of us at some point will struggle with worth. What does it mean? How shall we obtain it? And, will we pay the price to gain the worth? We may all chase worth differently and many of us will find it an illusory pursuit. The inescapable pull toward a life that matters and a work that endures challenges every one of us and a wrong response to that pull will blunt a life that matters. Where do we find our worth?

Some establish their worth on the hard stuff that they possess. For those who seek worth in this way, providing just for the basics no longer satisfies because just getting by suggests not getting on at all. Retailers have long noticed these cravings and marketed to them by offering easy-to-get credit cards, interest-delayed loans and low-down-payment mortgages as if the piper will never blow for them. The appeal to these cravings creates excitement and indecision as the consumer is overwhelmed with a diversity of products in colors, shades and designs to satisfy the growing American lust for a bigger, better, unique-to-you deal.

Even in religious endeavors, bigger seems better. The proposed cathedral for the Oakland diocese once had a budget of $190 million. The bishop suggests that such expensive facility will give "new energy" for the community. So goes the thinking that the larger the attendance in these brick and stone temples then the greater the critical mass and that translates into better worship. That better worship experience would then add worth to the one who engages in corporate public worship.

Many have adopted shopping as their national pastime and a means to worth. Every Saturday in America signs of garage, carport, yard and even estate sales go up. Not too many years ago, few consumers would walk into a concrete and metal warehouse to buy a month's worth of groceries and taste food at the sampling stations along the way or walk through aisle upon aisle of inviting media equipment for the best buy.

This shopping in the "big box" to get worth also has its contrasting "little box" companion. The "little box" offers more options and pricey ones in the niche marketing. Here a consumer can purchase a personally customized hot caffeine drink that distinguishes him from others. In these café oases, some workers sometimes identify to each other the customers by the distinguished drink that they order. "Here comes Mr. six shots, five Splenda latte man." Or, "Here comes Miss triple shot, half caf, non-fat, one-half raw sugar, and no foam latte lady." Then when the barista greets you, he or she finds out your name and puts it on your cup to publicly proclaim a relationship to the barista.

Others may identify worth with the stuff on their body because the culture promotes the external cage as a calling card and possibly even an idol. Folks may wear the right clothes, put on the attractive make-up and keep their hair in style to gain more than just the notice of others. Both men and women engage in expensive and sometimes unnecessary endeavors. Trainers make the body fit. Artists make the skin colorful and even textual.

Surgeons can expand parts of it and shrink other parts of it. This cultural body sculpting has its price and it also has its eventual demise. Los Angeles now has spawned tattoo removal shops.

A few others take the opposite view. They exalt their obesity such as the young woman who weighs 680 pounds and wants to set the world's record for a woman's weight by reaching 1000 pounds. She takes pride in her fat and sees fat as beautiful. She wants to encourage those other fat people who experience ridicule for their large beauty. Such an unhealthy and unbelievable obsession has sent interviewers to her doorstep to chronicle her bizarre quest for worth.

Entropy of all kinds ruins our stuff and our bodies. Every country experiences its economic cycles of "boom and bust." America has not escaped this rhythm. Many citizens forget or deny such rhythm because they may live to a very old age before a bust so affects them that their wealth no longer seems so robust. A failing economy curbs all these kinds of appetites. On the other hand, for those who live in the most "boom" times, they may think little about an economic failure until it comes.

No matter whether a person suffers because of a bust or rejoices because of a boom, that person could slip into the almost universal and illusory thinking that material possessions make one secure and that more possessions make one more secure.

When does worth begin? Some would argue that the acquisition of worth begins at birth. A child whose experiences give him a sense of relational attachment to significant others and especially parents enters adulthood with a healthy kind of worth as an adult and, as a bonus, with an ability to connect easily with others. On the other hand, if a person leaves childhood without this sense of worth, it may prove difficult to acquire later.

Many do seek worth in terms of internal or intrinsic worth, a sense of something other than financial security and something that cannot necessarily be seen. This kind of worth proves difficult in its definition and acquisition. This worth has its synonyms such as self-realization, self-identity or self-image.

Worth *Continuing*

We will all drift toward a bankrupt place when we live on a wrong assumption and we will have a wrong assumption if we refuse to have a true view of what matters and what has worth. Such drifting would pull us through an illusory pursuit that comes to a terminus at best of a wasted life and at the worst of a loss of life. We could be thinking that we have the correct basis of worth when we do not and we certainly cannot add worth to that which really has no worth. Such drifting must be aggressively thwarted since adding or multiplying worth to life does have legitimacy. We should all want to "live it up" in the sense of enjoying all that this life on earth offers according to its original design.

Certain questions can challenge our assumptions and accent the drifting. What kinds of pursuits translate into true worth? How ought we to understand what it means to multiply our worth? Finally, what stands as the most legitimate method toward worth?

Historians credit Harry Truman, the 33rd President of the United States with the phrase, "If you want to have a friend in Washington then get a dog." Today that may be true of so many of us because genuine loyalty and worthwhile conversation has gone out of style in relationships. We may not have a dog as a friend but what human friends that we have may have the loyalty of some dogs: the greater the chow or stuff from us, the greater the loyalty to us. And the blustery bark of most of our friends' support comes across as quite shallow with little bite of a true friendship. Ultimately, relationship marks the path to worth.

A unique kind of a relationship builds the cornerstone of worth in a person's life. Out of the root of this certain and particular kind of relationship grows the fruit of multiplied worth that provides meaning, freedom and hope. Such relationship molds character, gives meaning to life, grants significance and promotes the internal security that we all need. Only one kind of relationship can properly relate your work—what I do—to your identity—who I am. Before we explore this unique relationship let's examine some of the false pursuits of worth.

Part One: Worth Losing

The worn-out automobile expressed the owner's meaning of life in the sticker he had affixed to the scratched and beat-up bumper, "I live a much better life now that I have given up hope." If the driver of the automobile has truly given up hope, he has also by choice or most likely by default accepted a life of practical deadness because true hope enlivens and motivates. Philosophers may now solely occupy ground on the subject of meaning because people lack desire or they lack time or they are just plain too lazy to think about this defining matter of the meaning of life.

Who dares to stop when the day starts and ask, "Why am I really doing this anyway?" "How did I get to this point?" Or, more likely, we think, "How can I just get through this day?" More importantly, who answers his own questions of discovery and acts upon the results? Do we just leave the questions as rhetorical because we cannot face the answers to them? Most people have some sense of meaning even if it means to get up and be responsible enough to go to work each day. The grumbling cynic has some sort of meaning in his life of cynicism. Do we really think about the bigger picture beyond what we see and do? Do we just go along quietly and un-merrily piling up day after day sometimes quite monotonously until a sharp knot in the abdomen or a careening automobile or a sudden slip stops the streak of living days?

People no longer focus upon questions of purpose like: "Why have I been created?" "To what or to whom am I responsible?" "How can I escape the spiritual poverty or deadness of this life?" No longer in this culture does an understanding of our origin or a commitment to our design hold the reins of our lives and lead to responsibility. In any culture, affluence can bring a false sense of security, an illusion of belonging and a growing and willful disregard for what really matters. Benefit to self can dislodge benefit to others and the reflection in the bathroom mirror eventually reveals the aging image of one's worship.

The life of desire usually comes down nowadays to the life of personal economic profit and not just those in the historically affluent Western cultures. A connection to others comes only when others bring worth as defined by the personal profiteer. A return is expected from the relationship. Greed and selfish ambition derail any sort of calling or pursuit to an understanding of true purpose let alone an inclination toward altruism. Exceptions exist and we have seen their names in the newspapers and magazines of our day and we may be fortunate enough to know some; but, for most, worth is all about self and self's survival remains a paramount goal for those who seek to control.

Few have an outward let alone an upward focus. To define life by the question of "Will it add worth to me?" instead of "What purpose do I have?" has practical and eternal consequences. This modern self-centeredness, like an ancient and epidemic plague, will eventually hobble and shipwreck many of us.

The self-generated robbery and eventual destruction has to do with the nature of the pursuit. Lord Acton two centuries ago reminded all of us that "power corrupts and absolute power corrupts absolutely." The pursuit begins in a small way but its possession will eventually destroy any sense of a future hope or even of a developing character. Homer in *The Iliad,* said, "Such is the way the gods spun life for unfortunate mortals that we live in unhappiness, but the gods themselves have no sorrows." Homer's character only saw the happy ones as those who had absolute control. Many of us also practically do agree with that conclusion. We may not adhere to an ancient Greek view of little, powerless mortals and large, powerful gods; but, nonetheless, we will eventually find ourselves frustrated about the lack of control.

In spite of this frustration, we will continue in our pursuits for worth without recognizing our impotence in such pursuits. Let's summarize all these pursuits in four general categories: possessions, pleasure, prestige and people.

1

The Pursuit of Possessions

"Money is the answer to everything."
ECCLESIASTES 10.19B

The greed that gave the mythical king Midas the power of the golden touch to create his wealth also gave him the power to create his awful misery. His touch of power quickly turned his exquisite food, his beautiful roses and even his wonderful daughter into lifeless commodities with fabulous commercial worth. The gift to make gold had taken away his gift to make merry. The power that had given him stuff had destroyed his power to enjoy that stuff. As the Greek myth goes, at his request, the gods took away the gift that had stolen so much from him and restored his life and daughter to him. His desire for the power to have valuable possessions of extrinsic worth evolved into a curse that destroyed the living and valuable things of intrinsic worth.

Too many of us want something like the Midas touch but may eventually suffer from the effects of the Midas curse. Such curse begins quite small and innocently. You acquire new things and more things so that you gain efficiency but also maybe dependency. Take the power of the tools that you use to communicate. You may not need newer and better technology but because you can have the latest gadget, you want it. Your stuff may begin to define your life.

Where does the acquisition end? A device that keeps you more connected and gives ability to control more tasks will soon displace your now seemingly outdated device. 'Out of touch' implies 'out of control.' In spite of upkeep, entropy always wins. Hard drives crash; screens go blank and mobile phones go mute. You must fix or replace things when they break. That takes time and money to bring about the repairs or replacement. If they still work fine, you convince yourself that last year's device will not keep pace with this year's device. When that happens, you go from master to slave. As Thoreau said more than a century ago, "we become the tools of our tools."

You may also lose your stuff. Real storms such as a hurricane or tornado or a figurative storm such as personal bankruptcy or divorce can rob us of the stuff. We have all met such people after nature's devastation and seen the heartache on their faces about the loss of every personal belonging that may have taken a lifetime of work to acquire. Of course, an economic downturn robs the well-off and the not so well-off although the well-off and wise tend to survive. Also, later generations may expect the wealth of their parents or others to come to them without working for the wealth. Offspring can develop an attitude of entitlement. If stuff goes away for any reason, real and unjustified anger comes into play especially when others take away what you have earned or when you expect to be given what you have not earned and do not deserve.

The political freedom that America established also brings the economic freedom that Americans want. Developers recognize and provide places where freedom can exert its power to acquire and to relax. Malls still stand in another's phrase as "cathedrals of consumption." The Mall of America in Minnesota has a seven-acre camp for children and the mall occupies the space that could house eighty-eight football fields. With such large population of consumers, it also has its own police force that stays busy. Developers have popularized outdoor malls into which consumers drive, park and then walk. The shops sit around open green spaces that look like quaint villages that intend to give the ambience of an earlier and supposedly sweeter time in America.

The American dream of home ownership may rank as one of the larger stuff that folks possess. Many houses now have master bathrooms that would be half the size of houses in some parts of the world. Alarm systems abound because we do not want others to break in and to take our stuff. Rooms look like the designer's showplace or even a museum snapshot from life in America. Guests must marvel and compliment since they cannot sit.

I once had the privilege to interview a well-known American leader at his condominium in a downtown, river view high-rise. His gracious wife greeted us at the correct address and politely and immediately came outside to lead us next door to another condominium of slip covered furniture in pristine surroundings. Here in this second condominium, they entertained since, according to her, her famous husband just had too much stuff in their condominium where they lived to be hospitable to their many visitors. They could afford to meet others in this uncluttered one. On the other hand, how many folks maintain their home as a showroom that denies guests the hospitality that they need?

Stuff also leads to bigger houses and an additional storage area for your stuff. A garage no longer stores America's first love, the automobile, but all the stuff that the automobile brought home. Many Americans also purchase large houses not just to live in but for investment. These very large houses make for wise and popular purchases for family enjoyment now and profit later.

Just after the Iron Curtain fell, eastern Europeans, especially the formerly persecuted ones, could travel to America if they had a sponsor. On one occasion, a pastor from a previously controlled Soviet satellite nation left the airport with his sponsor who lived in one of these so-called McMansions. After the pastor entered the home and stopped in the expansive entryway with high ceilings and mammoth stairway, he politely asked his host, "How many families live in this building?" "My family," replied the host. Not long after that, whether from guilt or true desire, the host sold his house and moved on to live in a much simpler way—for a short time.

Everything from small miniature electric trains to large shiny automobiles and everything in between including books, coins, stamps, occupy the warehouses of collectors who take the name of picker or hoarder or connoisseur. A variety of cable programs document the lives of those who go out as "pickers" to uncover valuable stuff that others have purposely or inadvertently hoarded. Nothing lies beyond the grabber's reach. You find all kinds of collections: metal toy soldiers, plates, thimbles, light bulbs and celebrity paraphernalia like the tags the coroner used to mark the lifeless body of Elvis. A simple answer for a propensity to collect comes down to control. The collector enjoys the plastic, metal world that he has created. He rules over this fiefdom. Some people have so much stuff that a whole new career has arisen—the professional organizer. They even have their own group—the National Association of Professional Organizers. Worst of all, we have seen stories of those who have a hundred cats in their house or even a hundred snakes.

Eventually your stuff also begins to consume your thoughts. We slip from "I need [a necessity]" to "I want [a luxury]." "I possess; therefore, I am." Your stuff transforms itself into your idols. An idol acts as an object of worship and also as a thing of personal corruption because we were built to use stuff and not to be consumed by it. How do we keep our stuff from turning into idols? One sure sign has to do with the availability of your stuff to others. If you have a boat, would you let a friend take and operate the boat for his family on a weekend? Would you loan your truck to your brother-in-law? Would you let someone stay in your house in your absence even if it meant damage to furniture or house?

Over twenty-five years ago my family needed to travel almost cross-country to visit relatives. We planned on pushing all six of us into our vehicle. Instead, a friend loaned us his large, comfortable and brand new family vehicle to take that trip. Few folks had a Suburban truck or a "Texas Cadillac" as we called them in those days. Although only he could verify these thoughts, it seemed as if he kept that vehicle as stuff and had not transformed it into an idol. He taught me a critical lesson about the purpose of stuff and the worth of people.

Another friend had a similar lesson taught to him by his father. In high school, my young friend wrecked his small, brand new compact automobile on the way to high school. It could be driven but looked quite uncomplimentary with its dents and dirt. His father got to the scene to check on his son and surprised my friend by giving him the father's shiny, clean and expensive automobile to drive to school that day. As my friend drove off, he saw in his rearview mirror his banker father squeeze into the compact car with his expensive clothes and drive off in the damaged automobile. That moment gave my friend a lesson on stuff and a deeper love for his father.

We cannot forget the intangible stuff such as the so-called parchment paper from the university. Forty years ago, no high school sent 100 percent of its graduates to the university. Other options included trade schools or the armed forces. Today, a high school considers it a failure not to send 100 percent of its students to the university. Worst yet, parents consider it a failure if a child quits college. Furthermore, no longer does the basic degree give you enough status to get into the door of some companies. Today, to gain a bigger salary, a graduate must now go on and achieve one or two post-graduate degrees.

So-called educational mills take applicants money as they promise degrees just to complete some hours in their online studies. Certainly online classes have legitimacy but some schools operate as profit centers because they know that many students will pay and not continue in the program. Someone has estimated that the total loan repayment cost for all Americans for university education amounts to an estimate of one trillion dollars. This amount surpasses the total amount of credit card debt for Americans.

Stuff has a sense of power to it. It can control you for your detriment or you can control it for yours and others' benefit. The power to possess things reflects part of our human creativity but it also reflects part of our fallen humanity. Even the most successful or wealthy or most admired among us cannot escape the loss of stuff either.

Few of us have lived as the prodigious inventor and holder of over a 1000 patents Thomas Edison lived. In the evening of December 9, 1914, Edison stood on the property of his West Orange, New Jersey research facility as it burned down. He lost supplies, records, equipment and more with a cost of about $7 million in today's dollars. This spectacular fire did not go unnoticed as an incredible picture by Edison. He reportedly sent word to his family and friends, "Get down here quick....you may never have another chance to see anything like this again!" That night Edison began to sketch the design of his new facilities.

Possessions or stuff matters—up to a point. The simplest of inventions push our lives forward more efficiently. In this efficient push, as more stuff gives back more time, we have more time to consider the things that we could have. We also have time to acquire more stuff and that stuff begins to acquire a worth beyond its intended pragmatic design. These so-called hard things mean a lot to us not just to use and to enjoy but on which to capture worth. But do we dare to begin to measure our worth by what we have or what we do?

What about the Stuff that Destroys?

Pursuits of possessions or stuff that we ingest also consume our time and may consume our lives. According to the US Department of Commerce Americans consume about twenty-three pounds of candy a year per person and that excludes chewing gum and its relatives. Americans consume some 1.9 million Hershey chocolate candy bars a day. In 2011, $1.8 billion marked the total of tequila revenue in the United States. In 2007, some 80,000 students during spring break spent an estimated $2.5 million on alcohol just on South Padre Island, Texas.

Candy might harm your teeth or upset your stomach but other kinds of stuff could kill you. In a 2007 survey, forty percent of surveyed Americans over the age of twelve admitted to smoking marijuana at least once. At least two states have voted to legalize the distribution of weed. The late George Carlin slipped in on the television producers his salute of weed in his well-known skit of the *Hippy-Dippy Weatherman.* While many debate the effects of cannabis, Carlin got us to laugh at Al, his somewhat dazed meteorologist, because of his laid-back weather report. When Carlin delivered the following line, he did not refer to the high temperatures, "[it is] so hot that it would smoke the roaches." So-called insiders knew Carlin had little reference to the weather. In the slang of the American marijuana culture, "roach" refers to the blunt end of the marijuana joint or the brown paper left after smoking a joint. Supposedly more pleasure comes from the last part of the joint because more THC has accumulated there.

Some even brag about their use of marijuana. One of the "Ducks" of the University of Oregon football team that won the 2011 Rose Bowl said later in an interview in *ESPN Magazine*, "Some of us smoke [marijuana] and then we went out and won the Rose Bowl." One Duck star of the 1990's best expressed the way to survive the weather in Oregon, "Video games and weed."

The statistics on lethal or addictive stuff no longer shocks us. In February, 2012, four members of the TCU football team plus thirteen others were arrested for a drug ring. If you so desire, just browse any rural local paper and see the number of "meth" arrests that have taken place among those who you might think would not get involved in such harmful, risky behavior. According to a national survey, some 22 million Americans have some kind of drug or alcohol addiction. After marijuana, cocaine ranks as the second most commonly used illicit drug in the United States. More than 34 million Americans according to the National Survey on Drug and Health have used cocaine at least once in their lifetime. Some say that as many as 250,000 Americans have an addiction to heroine. Alcohol related deaths in 2009 in the United States exceeded over 30,000. Cigarettes can be linked to 40 per cent of all deaths from cancer.

Some 35 million Americans take antidepressants and antidepressant prescriptions are the third most prescribed drug in America. Five million Americans over the age of 50 have addiction to prescription drugs. When you consider that nine out of ten older Americans take a prescription drug every day, you can understand that Americans have fallen into prescription drug addiction. Another 300,000 deaths can also be attributed to obesity. An estimated 50 cents of every health dollar goes toward treating what health providers call health problems that find their source in lifestyle choices.

In affluent societies, luxuries may evolve into necessities. The latest gadget that gives the user the privilege to communicate quickly falls by the wayside when the owner expects to be entitled to a newer one. We have the privilege and the freedom to partake of all kinds of food and stuff but like King Midas we better not think that we can be entitled to a relief from the consequences of overindulgence.

Privileges that bring free stuff may evolve into entitlements. And those who receive these unearned entitlements freely may demand more entitlements or protest when others take them away.

The stuff that we possess cannot satisfy especially stuff that engenders an addiction that endangers life. Pursuit of stuff can also bankrupt us and possibly those around us. Stuff makes many of us feel good but stuff can deteriorate and can harm us. If the stuff that we see cannot stimulate us maybe the stuff that we can ingest will. Every nation has its history of economic "bust and boom" and meteorological disasters. When these tragedies happen (and they will) we could lose our possessions.

But, what would happen if in our pursuit of stuff we lose ourselves because our stuff begins to possess us?

How can one be immune from such a personal tragedy?

What worth do our possessions have if we fail to find the source of our true worth?

What does the ancient writer King Solomon say about stuff?

> *"As he came forth of his mother's womb, naked shall he return to go as he came, and shall take nothing from his labor, which he may carry away in his hand."* (Ecclesiastes 5.15)

2

The Pursuit of Pleasure

"I said in my heart, 'I will test you with pleasure to see if it has worth. So, enjoy yourself. Behold, it was futile."

ECCLESIASTES 2.1

In 1913, the Wrigley Company rolled out *Doublemint*. According to the company, the "double" came from the "double distillation" of the chicle or gum. The science of the double distillation would not advance sales like its advertisement that appeared in 1931 when the first art-enhanced twins showed up on highway billboards. In the 1960's the female twins and their male counterparts would expand sales with their television commercials where they proclaimed musically, "Double your pleasure; double your fun with *Doublemint* gum." This product still tops the sales for gum at Wrigley.

Who can deny the need for anyone, especially hard-working, highly committed individuals from taking a break from what they do—to have time for some pleasure? Today, many opportunities abound for Americans to more than double if not triple their pleasure.

Walt Disney and his "imagineers" as he called them took the pleasure of the amusement park to a previously unimagined level. They pioneered the concept of creating amusement parks around a theme of immersion. They would enhance the experience of the roller coast ride by putting it in a dark mountain or through an old mining town. They would give patrons more than rides; they would multiply the experience with so-called educational opportunities at the park. Presidents would talk; international dolls would sing of a small world; and nations would show their wares in their own little stores. His cartoon characters would magically appear on Main Street and delight visitors young and old.

The wonderful world began through an ersatz town with Disney workers who would dress as merchants to sell the Disney brands. Disney also had an advantage when the castle would splash right before your eyes before and after Disney's Sunday evening television show *The Wonderful World of Color.* Like the sirens that lured Ulysses, the kids of the 1950's watched that show and wanted to go to Disneyland and get that raccoon cap that Davey Crockett wore. Disney Inc. has continued to multiply their parks and their experiences of pleasure. By 2015, it will open Shanghai China in a country of 2300 amusement parks.

Theme parks, resorts and restaurants now abound in America and in the world to provide pleasure. The latest of these parks evolved from a series of best-selling books about a young wizard that Hollywood turned into motion pictures. Then, the movie company turned it into an amusement park that recreated the magical city of wizardry. On the first day that it opened, the line for admission took six hours just to enter. They created alluring areas for the freedom of pleasure in a recreated set of the city that the author imagined in the book and that the movie makers designed for the film. The vicarious experience also gives the visitor an opportunity to leave with a magician's wand instead of a faux coonskin cap or a gaudy tee shirt. How can you vacate from home unless you buy stuff to take home to remember your life-giving experience? How can you really enjoy the experience unless you take back home an artifact from that experience? Stuff later marks the experience as much as memories and pictures.

One particular place in America markets its appeal in a perverse way. It argues its appeal not just on the pleasure that you may have but on the privacy of that pleasure. At one point, some twenty years ago this city advertised itself as a place for the family with stage shows, water parks and of course, gaming [a euphemistic word for gambling]. Today, Las Vegas, a city with the most convention hotel rooms of any city in America stands by the motto, "What happens in Vegas stays in Vegas." No one can miss the point. While many say that they may be joking about the motto, they have found an engaging appeal for many conventioneers. The bright lights, faux fronts, and reduced copies of famous places in the world such as the Eiffel Tower make the gaming experience all too glamorous for many. After all, you can also go there to hear old and new entertainers. Families also still visit what others used to call "Sin City."

The American Gaming Association calculates that America now has 1200 casinos that employ approximately 400,000 workers. In 2005, approximately 73 million Americans visited a casino. In 2010, the twenty top casinos in America generated $25 billion in revenues. These statistics do not include the revenue totals from Native American casinos. Pari-mutuel betting fell in 2010 but still brought in revenues of $11.1 billion.

Gambling takes place legally in 48 states. Just in California in 2011, its lottery had sales of over $3 billion. Tennessee, a smaller state than California in terms of population, had record breaking revenue of $1.3 billion in 2012. Many Americans bet on-line although they could risk arrest for such a pursuit. Sports networks regularly promote the pleasure of gambling when they show gambling competitions. Sports show hosts speak of football point spreads and odds of winning in athletic contests.

Young athletes can find pleasure without going to Vegas. In the recent 2012 Olympics in London, every athlete received fifteen condoms which came in the colors of the Olympic rings. If you consider that some 10,000 athletes participated, that would mean a distribution of 150,000 condoms. After all, some say, why wouldn't these young and healthy specimens of physical excellence and mental discipline enjoy each other?

Others opt for beach vacations or cruises. The "Oasis of the Seas" can carry a maximum of 8,600 passengers and staff. Its length measures almost four football fields and advertises twenty-four restaurants, a leafy "central park," climbing wall, zip line, surf pool, and twenty-four hour laundry. It takes on at least 750 pallets of food which includes 20 gallons of maraschino cherries just for the bars. *Corona* beer tops the list of the most ordered beer.

Pleasure, like any addiction, has a dark side to it. You might go into debt to pay for such pleasure. You might even injure yourself on a ride or, like the occasional cruise ship, find yourself shipwrecked like the Costa Concordia that went aground in the Mediterranean in January 2012 and killed at least six people. Or, you could develop an addiction to gambling. The National Council on Problem Gambling estimates that 4 to 6 million Americans are "problem gamblers." Most importantly, you could die from the pursuit of pleasure.

On November 7, 1991, Magic Johnson, a noted NBA all-star and eventual member of the Hall of Fame, revealed his HIV positive status. Up until that point, the American media regarded those with HIV as less respected, blameworthy, and maybe even malefactors. But this NBA player does not hold the record for the first athlete to have HIV from a pursuit of pleasure.

The one who would receive that tragic and unenviable record arose out of an unexpected arena: the National Association of Stock Cars. NASCAR allegedly birthed itself on the engine blocks of moonshiners who had to be fast and ingenious to outwit and outrace the revenuers. Eventually, these southerners would take a break from their deliveries of white lightning and race against each other on Sundays in vacant fields. In some way, NASCAR epitomized so much of early America: independence, adventure and family loyalty. As one observer has noted, this circuit of primarily southern audiences in the early days consisted of "good ole boys, rednecks and their women."

In the 1980's NASCAR gained a greater allegiance beyond the South as television brought its swagger into the Sunday afternoon living rooms. Into that traditional and early context came a racer whose off track race clothes reflected more of Wall Street than southern race Tee shirt casual and whose lifestyle reflected more of Hollywood [where he spent his off season time with movie stars] and a whole lot less of Talladega campgrounds. As far as his track life went, even the late Dale Earnhardt who had the fitting moniker of "the Terminator" characterized this stylish fellow as aggressive and competitive in a stock car. In fact, in his first year, NASCAR awarded "Rookie of the Year" honors to this new competitor by the name of Tim Richmond.

His team owner recognized his immaturity and gave Richmond a seasoned, crusty team chief. Others began to recognize this disparate mix as a team to beat as a formidable opponent on the track. After he concluded successfully the 1979 season, Richmond sat out the next one because of illness. Others had begun to notice his regular coughing in post-race interviews and his less than notable racing. Racing insiders and outsiders suspected drug use. They thought they had the right conclusion when he returned the next year to race but failed the drug test not due to anything but an abundance of over the counter drugs.

At that point, Tim Richmond returned to his parents' vacant condominium in Florida, sat his equipment bag on the counter for the last time, entered a darkened bedroom and experienced pain and depression for the final six months of his life. In his final days, as the now emaciated no longer youthful looking athlete later lay dying in a hospital, his attendants had no idea of his driving success until they saw the television tribute before a NASCAR race.

On 13 August 1989, sometime after he saw the tribute to himself, Richmond died. His friends back in Ohio would later honor him with a toast and say, "Oh how he lived!"

Until then no one associated with NASCAR could have imagined that this attractive tall athlete could die at age 34 especially of AIDS. He had no history of blood transfusion or wanton homosexuality but Hollywood told of his numerous relationships with women.

The bluesy alcoholic Southern Comfort drinker Janis Joplin at age 27 died alone in a seedy West Coast hotel. As she said, "Look, I'm not a spokesman for my generation. I don't use acid. I drink." She reveled in the excesses of her life whether it came from sex or alcohol. Brian Jones, Rolling Stones guitarist, left his lifeless body on the bottom of a pool from drug and alcohol excess. Jimi Hendrix of Woodstock and "Purple Haze" fame who promoted LSD, marijuana, and cocaine died at age 24 of a drug overdose.

Both Jim Morrison of the Doors and Elvis Presley had official death causes as heart failure. While Morrison lived a life of excessive alcohol use, the bodyguards of Elvis said this about Elvis, "He is a walking pharmaceutical shop. He takes uppers and downers and all sorts of very strong painkillers, Percodan and the stuff they give terminal cancer patients. Yes, he knows a lot about drugs." They could guard him from others but they could not protect him from himself. The Jefferson Airplane spoke about drugs' effects when they sang, "One pill makes you larger. One pill makes you small…"

Observers might disingenuously argue that pressure caused them to possess and take such stuff into their bodies. The prestige that they desired in terms of audience approval may have brought them and/or their possessions to an end. Today, just in prescription drugs alone, Americans spend around $307 billion annually. As to prescription use, almost fifty per cent of Americans take at least one prescription drug a month. Additionally, some estimate almost twenty two million Americans have addiction to illegal drugs.

Pleasure like possessions has its boundaries. Whether we like it or not, pleasure has its price. That price might come in the simple form of too much double pleasure that brings decay to our teeth. Or, it could come in the injurious form of gambling addiction or in once forbidden sexual pleasures that could harm oneself or one's family.

The kind of worth that pleasure brings cannot be a worth that lasts.

You may not be one that has succumbed to too much pleasure or the wrong kind of pleasure. You may not be the one who lives life for your possessions. But have you pursued prestige to gain worth?

3

The Pursuit of Prestige

"They put your name on a star on Hollywood Boulevard and you find a pile of dog manure on it. That's the whole story, baby!"

LEE MARVIN (1924-1987) ACTOR

We cannot doubt the late beekeeper's account of the ascension. The debate about which one got to the top first does not tarnish the remarkable accomplishment that man had finally ascended to the top of the world. On May 29, 1953, Edmund Hillary and Tenzing Norgay wedged their way through a forty foot crack, climbed a bit more and stood on the peak of Everest at 29,028 feet to be declared the first to make successfully the climb, get down and have it verified. Others like George Mallory had tried and failed. Mallory, the British climber who lost his life in ascending Everest in 1924, receives credit for the four word mantra of mountaineers. In response to the question "Why do you want to climb Mt. Everest?" He answered, "Because it is there." That would not be the end of Hillary's life because the prestige of that climb would bring money, greater status and even a knighthood from the Queen for this Kiwi climber. This mountain conquering beekeeper would go on to mark achievements in such areas as the environmental conservation, philanthropy and education.

Since that day over two thousand climbers have ascended into these mountains that Buddhists consider sacred. Thousands more have ascended just to the base camp to take supplies. Many others have ascended to the same base camps to bring back the discarded canisters and other trash. Two hundred climbers have paid the price of a loss of life because of an unabated ambition to put one foot in India and another in Nepal at the top of the world. The most well-known tragedy on this almost five mile mountain took place on 10-11 May 1996 when eight died and accusations abounded about who caused the death of some very qualified and experienced mountain climbers.

Once you have seen the world from the top of its highest mountain, what else amazes you?

Prestige finds its origin in the French language where its etymology means "illusion." If a sleight of hand artist performed a most difficult of tricks, it might be called the "prestige." It comes into the English language as a word for the weight or credit that a person receives in the eyes of others. Few have lost their lives in the practice of a magical illusion but how many have lost their lives in the pursuit of prestige? Too many times, prestige for some has no validity. Vaclav Havel, past president of the Czech Republic, said it in this way, "[We live] in a world of appearances trying to pass for reality."

You can acquire prestige in a variety of ways. Over two hundred years ago, Adam Smith, the Scottish economist, commented on the nature of clothes and what it said about you. A man who could wear a linen shirt instead of a coarse itchy woolen shirt suggested that he had enough money to wear such clothes. The linen shirt suggested an elite status.

Over fifty years ago, America created something more important than a linen shirt for prestige. Henry Ford had the right business idea about the American automobile; people needed a cheap means of transportation. In the 1960's, the World Series and introduction of new automobiles marked the true beginning of autumn in a car-crazy America. Lee Iacocca made Ford competitive again when the Mustang debuted with much hurrah and buyer acceptance on April 13, 1964 some six months ahead of the normal sales cycle.

Iacocca built on Henry Ford's idea of availability. He promoted this Pony class of automobile as an inexpensive but prestigious metal icon. It did not stop there. While the cultural elites push for their green means of transportation, automobile manufacturers still sell prestige with automobiles and trucks that cost what houses used to cost. Of course, the owners also get to argue that the reliability and safety of the automobile justify the sticker price.

In the marketplace in terms of prestige, the status of a job may rank higher than the wages of a job. An MBA from Harvard could open a door more quickly than an MBA from somewhere else. Whether Harvard deserves the creditability or not it has that status. Reality television gives prestige to the least of us in terms of meaningful contributions and such undeserved status could lead to the achievement of money.

In the political arena, an assumption of prestige ranks high in attracting voters. A supposedly happily married politician achieves a high status because of a strong speech about morality. Then his pregnant girlfriend appears and his worth to the party and his electability has diminished or goes to zero. A respected leader falsifies his war record and must confess his obfuscation lest he lose his public office. An impeached President holds on to his prestige by distorting and lying about his many peccadilloes.

In that political arena, prestige takes on the synonym of gravitas. Gravitas equals political clout. Vietnam War military experience has suddenly gained national status as a prestige producer. A Presidential candidate who opposed the war immediately after he returned in testimony to Congress later touted his purple hearts and service in Vietnam to win votes among veterans in the population. He switched his source of prestige from being the one who told the truth about Vietnam to being the one who had served well enough in Vietnam to be injured. The sources of prestige can shift even if it shifts on the same person.

Even the most successful or wealthy or most admired among us cannot stop pursuing stuff that brings prestige. Every athlete in the National Football League wants to participate in and win what Lemar Hunt, the late owner of the Kansas City Chiefs, dubbed the Super Bowl. When any player whose team wins the game gives an interview, no one asks about what he received in terms of money. Instead, the conversation revolves around the ring. Each winning team has custom-made rings whose artwork fits their team and its victory. That ring brings prestige when someone sees it on that player.

The New Orleans saints in 2010 won Super Bowl XLIV. Each player's ring had forty-four diamonds on it; one side had the score, date and location of the contest;

and the other had the player's name with landmark and notes that would identify the ring with New Orleans. On top rested the fleur-de-lis, the symbol for the saints. The football league will pay up to $5000 for each ring although some sources say that this gift to each winning player could run as high as $20,000. When the San Francisco Giants won the World Series in 2002, each championship ring had 77 diamonds and each weighed a little less than a carat. The great Yankee legend and quipster Yogi Berra commented on these rings, "You can't believe how big these rings are today. They're not rings; they're weapons."

Players talk about the ring because of its prestige. Jason Terry, member of the 2011 NBA champion Dallas Mavericks, played 12 seasons before he received a ring. He said this about the worth of the ring: "Once you get that ring you know that you're a champion. You have to have that piece and you can show it to the entire world. If you go up to someone and you shake their hand and they see that ring, it changes things." The idea that a ring "changes things" suggests the power of stuff when it reflects prestige or fame.

Sometimes, a lifestyle of pleasure leads to the loss of a possession of prestige. Rick Harrison, star of the TV show *Pawn Stars* knows all about prestige. He meets people who enjoyed the high life who now live in the low of their lives. He has regularly purchased from desperate people all kinds of items: necklaces, watches, gold pieces, automobiles, rare weapons. However, when he can purchase an Olympic medal or a boxing title belt, he knows that he could double his investment when he sells it.

He even brags about having a genuine Super Bowl ring in his possession. As he says, "You want the thing a guy worked his whole life on to get." The sports world of journalists and fellow teammates make public their lament when some former Super Bowl winner or an Olympic champion has to pawn his ring or medal because the good times of wealth have left him and he must sell his metal prestige.

Prestige takes no break from education either. On one television news program, a journalist dealt with the issue of college education and its cost. One interviewee spoke of the stress of providing education for her three children, "It will cost $40,000 a year and we have three children; I am going to be working for a long time to pay for them to go to college." Certainly, other universities would not cost as much or possibly could educate as well as these elite schools to which her children applied. In spite of the truth of such statement, the interviewee suggested that no other school could open the doors that this school would open. Could it be that when friends hear of her children in these elite schools, will others think more highly of her and her husband?

Many years ago during another economic downside, an acquaintance of mine shared with me his financial misfortune as a purveyor of bonds. He had made money for a long time with a minimum amount of work and then one day the market collapsed for him. He found it difficult to keep his children in private school and had to send his wife to work to pay some of the bills. None of that seemed to bother him as much as his failure to give to his local church. The amount that he gave did not bother him so much as the knowledge that others would know that he could no longer pay his former tithe. He could have given something if giving seemed so important to him. He decided to give nothing until he could give a larger amount that reflected his former tithe lest he lose his prestige or standing with others who might discover his giving amount.

Prestige from a self-centered point of view can also be defined as your network. Young people may speak about degrees of relationship. If you have a relationship with a person whose best friend happens to be the friend of a well-known person who carries status or prestige, then you stand very close to the prestige of the well-known person.

Sometimes and possibly eventually even legitimate prestige can fade. Every American war winds down at some point. After the Vietnam conflict, former helicopter pilots and other officers endured the RIF (reduction in force). Others had to retire to squeeze the Army to so-called peacetime levels. These officers would walk in one day to be greeted with respect and assumed authority because of the uniform that they wore. They would return in their civilian clothes the very next day to pick up their papers and be treated quite casually. For many they accepted that their season of service had passed. For those who were ready to be released, they found relief. For those who could not face life in civilian attire, they found anxiety.

When my colonel retired after 22 years, he sensed and illustrated that abrupt departure. The Army had provided him the uniform, ribbons and brass that demanded respect. The very next day he had to put on the everyday rayon and cotton of ordinary civilians. He would now receive no necessary and immediate human respect because of the externals that demanded respect. Instead of a uniform that would make the man, the man had to make himself.

No astronaut died at the moon or on the way to the moon; but, three astronauts died on the ground in the program that would be a step to get men to the moon. Most know the memorable allegedly spontaneous words, "One small step for man—one giant leap for mankind." Twelve men have walked on the moon, but who can remember any astronaut beyond the first one, the late Neil Armstrong?

Some people wear their prestige. Other than being lost at sea, a mother used to fear that her young son would return with a tattooed arm. Today, "inked up" folks abound. The parlor of the tattoo artist has moved from the seedy Skid Row locales to Main Street America. Fraternity and sorority members maintain their Greek prestige with the ink of their membership on ankles. Athletes used to wear some sort of barbed wire look on their biceps. Now, anything goes. No economic class finds itself immune from this skin prestige. This inked prestige has come a long way from Popeye's anchor on his bicep.

You do not have to do much to achieve prestige in the popular culture. You could appear on television in a most inane setting and then have prestige. You could be the last survivor on a reality television show. You could put a picture or a quote of no more than 140 characters on social media and gain some degree of prestige. A person can win a lottery and gain instant prestige and unwanted re-acquaintance with some lost or formerly estranged relatives.

Achievement does mean walking on the moon, climbing Mt. Everest, earning an Eagle badge, succeeding at a business plan or giving away earnings in philanthropy toward others. Those kinds of pursuits could bring you a legitimate prestige because prestige could come later when people recognize the hard work that brought you success.

College students certainly join sororities and fraternities for future connections and college status but they also join for a sense of belonging no matter how small the belonging or how high the price. They can now have worth and maybe multiplied worth because they belong to a smaller and hopefully more recognizable group at the university.

In the marketplace of adult life, adults also find 'tribes' that they may join. You might think that all this desire to belong ends after college but singles may gather to identify with others by the same dress, the same gathering place or smoke the same kind of legal or illegal substances. Slick and efficient hand-held devices help to keep the tribe on the perpetual merry-go-round of "being in touch" and available to gather at a moment's notice. Others may join all kinds of civil and religious organizations in their communities to have a sense of belonging. Many take the very straightforward and traditional approach of preparing for and achieving a profession that has built-in status or group identity. The simple step of meeting with your informal tribe, earning the right to wear a club's identifiable moniker or taking the right job may not bring belonging or even intimacy. In spite of such push, too many of us never connect with others in spite of the desire to do so in spite of the illusion that constant superficial communication implies genuine deep connection.

Even in death, people want their prestige or fame to continue. Al Jolson, the "world's greatest entertainer" [in his time] has a burial crypt at Hillside Memorial Park in Culver City, California not far from the freeway. Water continually flows downward from his memorial; a bronze statue stands in the midst of the hillside columns and he continues to sing through his recorded music via loud speakers. Evelyn Y. Davis, the self-proclaimed "Queen of the Corporate Jungle," has been working on her grave monument for thirty-one years. The eighty-two-year-old protector of stockholders of corporations concluded that no one else would put on the granite tombstone what she wanted. As she says, "I'm interested in immortalizing my name." Maybe that will do it; but, maybe others will forget in spite of the large side panels that list her accomplishments and sayings like, "Power is greater than love, and I did not get [to] where I am neither by standing in line nor by being shy."

Nations also struggle with prestige. On March 2, 1969 the French supersonic transport plane took off and flew for thirty-five minutes. When the so-called beautiful bird took to flight that day, the assembled crowds shouted *Allez France! Allez France!* The French magazine *Le Monde* commented that the Concorde "was created largely to serve the prestige of France." Somehow this government built taxpayer funded plane would return the nation of France to its place of status and respect in the world of nations. Thirty one years later as Air France 4590 ascended from the runway, the Concorde blew a tire and unceremoniously and tragically crashed into a vacant building in Paris. The lost lives included one hundred Germans in a tour group, nine crew members including six flight attendants and four bystanders. As it fell so did the prestige of French engineering.

The French had overlooked practical objections. Even an excellent pilot had to be constantly alert to fly it. One pilot commented that "there are about fifty reasons besides engine failure" to require an emergency landing. In spite of the speed of the super plane, investors chose not to come forward as needed. Many cities refused to let it land because of the noise of its engines on take-off. The sonic boom kept it from flying profitable routes like New York to Los Angeles. The engines used an inordinate amount of fuel compared to other jets and in a time when fuel had risen dramatically. To keep the center of gravity proper, fuel had to be moved manually around its fourteen tanks.

In spite of fifty-seven tire related accidents and thirty-two blowouts that damaged the plane in some way, the French aviation authorities overlooked the close disasters. They also overlooked repetitive incidents of lost parts of elevators and rudders in flight. They kept the plane flying for thirty-one years despite objections until the fatal crash ended its life and grounded the thirteen other ones of British Airways and Air France. In spite of testimony to the contrary, Continental Airlines took the blame and paid the families because a metal strip had fallen off its plane at the takeoff just before the Concorde's flight. The French did not lose their case but they lost their prestige and at the highest of prices. No longer could they proclaim because of this plane, "Go France!"

The power of prestige, that power to gain from others a sense of importance or a sense of exalted position, could kill you or others. For those who perished on Mt. Everest or who perished on the Concorde, what prestige that they had they can no longer enjoy on this earth. Metal icons will break down; tattoos cannot overcome wrinkles; and honors will fade.

Can the possession of prestige give us a lasting worth? Those three hundred some Sherpa who carried 10,000 pounds up the mountain for Hillary achieved something but they probably gained no prestige. Only twelve men have stepped foot on the moon. The teams at Canaveral and Houston worked long hours for the achievement to send and bring back those astronauts but they gained little prestige. Less than fifty men have ever held the office of President of the United States but who worked and paid to get them there?

Prestige does have it many pursuers. Like the origin of the word in the French language, prestige comes as an illusion. Earthly worth remains vulnerable because stuff, pleasure, titles, jobs and successes do not last. Certainly, when affirmations fade and connections with others fail, a person may suffer some kind of identity malnutrition. In that case, those who seek worth in the extrinsic sense may not die physically but inside they suffer because they sense a lack of worth.

What else could we pursue to solve this problem of worth?

4

The Pursuit of People

"No man is an island entire of itself."

JOHN DONNE, ENGLISH POET

At the climax of the third Indiana Jones motion picture, "Indiana Jones and the Last Crusade," the artifact rescuer Indiana and the Nazi villain reach the hidden cave where for centuries an aged Crusader has protected the Holy Grail that Jesus and the disciples supposedly drank from at the Last Supper. As the plot goes, a drink of holy water from the Holy Grail brings a life of eternal youth.

To their dismay, in the cave sits a long table with an assortment of many goblets in a variety of composition and decorations. The villain naturally chooses the most ostentatious cup and it turns out to be the wrong cup. After he drinks, he immediately grows older and dies in a horrifying, cinematic presentation that only puppeteers, time-lapse photography and computer generated graphics could bring to the viewer. The aged crusader then says in a dead pan way without any emotion about the villain, "He chose poorly."

Now Indiana chooses. He thinks out loud about the humility of the Carpenter and picks a rather ordinary and plain goblet. He drinks, survives, and rushes out quickly through the formerly dangerous passageway to save his dying father whom the Nazi villain had wounded. He pours the life-giving water from the goblet upon the wound of his father and he recovers. The crusader says this of Indiana, "You chose wisely."

Choice marks out our humanity.

Every year for about three months at the end of one calendar year and the beginning of another over one million Americans, mostly men, rise early, put on their usually expensive, warm, camouflaged clothing; pull on their hip boots and with well-trained dogs head out into the cold to sit in sunken pits, stand in shallow waters or occupy a boat and wait. If the weather cooperates, the sky will reward their perseverance. Around 775 species of North American birds migrate every year. So many waterfowl migrated in 1995 that some Midwest air traffic controllers could not distinguish these dense flocks from airplanes in this historic "grand passage."

These birds make no conscious effort to choose to enter this "killing zone" where humans have disguised the water below as a safe and nutritious landing. Their biological clock has sent them south to survive as they look for favorable habitats on their way to escape the cold of the north. No one really understands the mystery of their departure or in their ability to regularly orient themselves to navigate the 2300 miles of this sky highway. In the last century waterfowl hunters gathered together and formed organizations to insure that more generations of hunters after them could enjoy their pursuit by limiting hunting times, limiting hunting places and maintaining favorable habitats. In all of these measures, no bird registered an opinion or had an opportunity to vote.

Duck hunters make choices that ducks cannot make and some spouses may not like. Certainly many birds sense danger and land elsewhere or others just escape due to poor shooting. Those who by nature walk on the earth could choose to exercise their power to deny life to those who by nature have the power to soar above the earth. The power to kill overcame the power of the birds to fly and to escape.

Why do we pursue others?

The pursuit of people marks out our humanity. When you sign up for *Google+*, they ask you to choose your circle of friends. They suggest that you pick "your real friends, the ones you feel comfortable sharing private details with." Facebook has over one billion users. More than half of its users log in at least once a day. This average rises upward among 18-to-34 year olds. Internet organizations like E-Harmony want to help you connect with others who might want to spend part of their life with you. Who can count the number of text messages that high school students send to each other throughout the day? It used to be that punishment for the teen meant room confinement but now it means removal of the mobile phone where young teens [and others] live. Can you walk through a parking lot or store and not see people talking on or fiddling with their phones as they walk?

Social networks connect people with each other in a distant way. Being well-connected electronically does not mean that you are well-related intimately. No phone-to-phone text can replace face-to-face talk. Many Americans live alone, act independently and feel lonely. Sadly, too many Americans also die alone without any close friends or family nearby. Social networks really promote a pseudo or fake intimacy. While we cannot fault companies who promote these ersatz relationships and certainly do it for a profit, they cannot create true intimacy. That may explain the success of a company like Skype that lets you see the face of the person as you talk to them. Communication that leads to intimacy takes more than just the words. As someone has said, communication today puts as much emphasis on "how" you say it and not just on "what" you say. That takes face to face contact.

When we speak of the pursuit of people, that pursuit comes naturally in our DNA. We are born with a desire to be close to others. Observers have chronicled the difficulty that infants have to thrive or later connect with others intimately if no one holds them and/or talks to them as infants. World War II left Europe with many orphans who failed to connect with other human beings. A whole new theory arose to describe this phenomenon: attachment theory. If a person has no primary care-giver in childhood, that person may fail later to maintain relationships with others as an adult. Those who fail to do this have "attachment issues." The theory has gained more public discussion now than after World War II because so many folks seem to have a problem with getting close to others. Young adults may see that their inability to connect with others is sourced in their emotional abandonment by fathers or mothers in their formative years.

Intimacy does not come immediately or naturally. It has no particular formula but we must be in others' presence to really know them. Although we are designed to live our lives in community with other human beings, we are beginning to act in this culture as if we can only know each other best when we have the safety of digital distance between us.

Who makes what choices?

Two competing and contrasting approaches define the pursuit of people: those who take from others and those who give to others. We all probably fall in and out of the two contrasting styles depending on circumstances and choices. Maybe no one stays in one class all the time.

Takers can gain worth in legitimate and morally acceptable ways. They prove their worth by being successful at what they do although that could mean controlling everything around them and that includes people. Fans appreciate the well-disciplined athlete who competes to win the prize. These athletes work at their profession and anyone who survives as a winner will gain further worth as others applaud and appreciate them beyond their chosen field of play. Fans will appreciate and rejoice over the success on the field, court, or track of their favorite athlete or team. Some fans even gain a sense of worth by wearing the jersey of their favorite player.

Others take their worth from people in a vicarious and usually innocent way. Entertainers attract those who pursue them and piggyback on them for their worth. These followers wear clothes like their favorite entertainment idol wears. By looking like their idols or collecting stuff of their idols, they have a weird sense of worth by belonging to something much bigger than themselves. Tabloids over the years speak of the so-called "groupies" who follow rock stars.

Elvis Presley had his TCB ["Taking Care of Business"] mafia or posse of tightly-knit friends who could help him hide out to relax to escape from his responsibilities. He would rent whole theaters or a local amusement park just for him and his close friends. The members had worth because their leader had worth. If you really got close enough to Elvis, you might receive jewelry in the shape of the letters "TCB." Elvis seemed to accept and to want these friends around him and maybe that gave him in return a sense of worth.

People still seek out Elvis. Throughout the year, thousands from all over the world will visit Graceland, the former home of Elvis. In August, during the so-called "Dead Week" by local Memphians when fans come in droves to commemorate his death, some will dress like Elvis, maybe wear fifties type clothes and even weep at his grave. This macabre sense of pursuing a dead man to gain worth baffles many.

On the other hand, in our pursuit of people, our choices have not been kind to one another. We have all known or read about those individuals who return to their office to do harm to their office mates. Sometimes those who feel the brutality of a bully return to take revenge on that bully. You can go all the way back to the Hebrew writing where Moses records the death of Abel by Cain out of jealousy. Cain hated the results of his choices but blamed his brother for blunting Cain's expectations. The phrase 'raising Cain' refers to someone who acts out of control. The phrase ought to remind each of us of that violent moment where a choice in anger brought about the death of another person.

In terms of control many of us think and may act like Cain. Instead of serving those whom we pursue and hopefully love we attempt to gain happiness for them and for us by control. Marital counselors pinpoint this issue of control as one of the frustrations that women have in their marriages. The husband tries to protect his wife by controlling environment and circumstances with the thought that she would feel safe. Instead, she feels angry and disrespected. In a sane framing, no one has permission to choose to harm another intentionally except for self-defense. Hunters may be free to choose to harm ducks but we should not choose to harm others in our pursuit of them.

John Hinckley Jr. acted as a taker when he pursued the actress Jodie Foster. On March 30, 1981, he created his own killing field outside of the Washington Hilton as he took the opportunity to shoot President Ronald Reagan. He somehow thought that he could impress Jodie Foster. He wanted to take the life of one to gain a relationship to another. Such magical thinking put him in prison but not the death chamber due to his defense of insanity.

On April 20, 1999, two high school boys walked into their school to set off explosives to trap some fellow 600 students and murder them if they tried to escape. Some considered the boys' victimization by bullying as the cause of their murderous actions. Harris and Klebold had much bigger motives as investigators later discovered. They wanted to take the lives of fellow students to gain a worth of prestige by gaining the title as two of the greatest killers in history. They considered Attila the Hun their idol as they chose in a pre-meditated, well-thought way to murder their fellow Columbine students. Their pursuit ended in their own deaths by suicide after they murdered thirteen and injured another twenty-four fellow students.

These kinds of examples ought to sicken us. We cannot imagine that evil of this kind can exist especially among young people but it does. We continue to experience multiple murders since then. Most Americans know of the killings at Virginia Tech or Sandy Hook Elementary School. As of 2010, according to the magazine *Mother Jones,* America has witnessed 61 mass murders since 1982.

The FBI defines mass murder as any murders at the same time in the same place with four or more deaths. Many single murders often take place among family members or people who know each other. Reports of murder may no longer shock us because it leads the news daily and that's cause for mourning.

In sharp contrast, others gain worth by giving to people. Those who give money, time and abilities continue to be part of the American character. Colorful bows, shirts and other paraphernalia mark out those who give to different service organizations. The smallest towns in America sponsor a 5K family walk or race to benefit a needy family or worthy organization. Pink has acquired new meaning as cancer researchers now benefit from the displayed color. Who could have predicted that professional football players would wear bright pink somewhere on their uniform?

In 2007, Americans gave a record $307 billion to charity. This figure would exclude churches, synagogues and mosques. The Salvation Army during its "Red Kettle" Christmas season raised around $150 million in 2010. St. Jude's Research Hospital received approximately $728 million in donations in 2011. We cannot account for all the money and time that individuals gave to helping victims of storms, building homes for the less fortunate or any other similar pursuits. We cannot forget those who choose to risk their lives every day to give to others such as firefighters, police officers, soldiers, sailors and marines.

The terrorist attack on America on September 11, 2001 forced pilots of oceanic flights to divert and land immediately in the closest runway not in the United States. Thirty-nine pilots landed their diverted equipment in Gander, Newfoundland, a small town that had an international airport on the most northeastern point of North America. The citizens of Gander and those of the province of Newfoundland provided housing, food and comfort for 6,579 passengers in and around this town of some 10,000 people. They improvised shelters; they opened their homes; and they provided other needed items. They offered their showers, their beds and even shared their prescription drugs. Some townspeople even bought birthday presents and put on a party for a youngster. Ten years later some of these comforted and stranded passengers returned to thank townspeople. Other former passengers have developed relationships with these givers who responded to the need.

The pursuit of others could be the most satisfying of all pursuits if we act as givers. Mother Teresa of Calcutta stands out among many other noted historical figures that appeared to find satisfaction on earth in giving to others. But, who could persevere as she did especially in the darkest of her hours when no one cared and she knew that she could not save everyone? In spite of the noble desire to give, even givers will find themselves in the same bankrupt place as takers without an overall view that identifies the motive for their giving.

Nonetheless, when it comes to pursuing people will we act as duck hunters and treat others as prey or will we act as an Indiana Jones and treat people as valuable treasure?

Worth Thinking

Following pursuits comes as part of being human. These four pursuits may not capture every person's philosophy of life but they appear to be the fundamental choices of many of us. From the moment of birth, we naturally continue to look outward and to focus beyond ourselves. We cannot escape the way that we have been built. Since we were born to pursue, we will pursue something or someone until others or death stops us.

In spite of our propensity to pursue, honest folks know that these pursuits cannot finally satisfy because they only last temporarily. Possessions will decay; pleasures will pass; prestige will fade and people will die.

In spite of temporary satisfaction, we can characterize these pursuits as successful and rewarding if we have a proper narrative, true grid or world-view to interpret and govern our pursuits. Otherwise, these pursuits only "fix us" temporarily with satisfaction. This pursuit of worth brings up questions like:

* *How will a world-view govern my pursuits?*

* *How will this overall narrative satisfy?*

* *How will a true narrative give a sense of purpose that I lack?*

* *Will something or someone keep me from gaining such a view?*

* *How is a world-view connected with real worth?*

Before we discuss the concept of world-views, let's look at some preliminary thoughts prior to looking at the particular world-view or assertion that this book presents

5

The Trouble with Truth

"But you've gotta make your own kind of music
Sing your own special song
Make your own kind of music
Even if nobody else sings along"

MAMA CASS ELLIOTT, 1969,
MAKE YOUR OWN KIND OF MUSIC

Pontius Pilate, that vilified and self-interested Roman political ruler did not coin the phrase although he takes notoriety for it. Many others had asked it before him whether in mockery or in earnest. Moreover, it can eventually be found somewhere deep within everyone's mind and not just in the minds of the philosophers: "What is truth?" The answer to this question about truth leads to the very foundations of all that we are and all that we do. Prior to very recent changes in courtroom procedure, a witness would have to affirm this oath, "Will you swear to tell the truth—the whole truth—so help you God?"

When it comes to the practical part of everyday life, no sane person purposely denies the truth by opposing it. Airplanes must land on runways or crash. Without water a person will die. Only a rocket can escape gravity and not forever. In other areas such as the unseen and the supernatural, most of us don't care much for the truth these days. Like the muddy pig, we just take mud for granted and live oblivious to the lies that we believe.

We ought to have reasons to believe what we do. When it comes to a proposition that involves money or a relationship of permanence with another such as marriage, a person ought to have the truth. We may be afraid of the truth; but, without the truth, how can we live purposely and safely? Without the truth about an economic adventure, the money will be lost. Without the truth about others to whom we commit ourselves, the relationship cannot survive. Without the truth about danger, we could lose our lives.

Researchers spend their lives and other peoples' money to find out the truth about cancer or AIDS or cardiovascular disease to find a cure for others. Many of these same bright and highly educated folks look like the rest of us when they fail to spend the time or the energy to find out the truth about matters that concern life and God.

Trustworthiness and truth go hand in hand. We ought not to trust what proves to be untrue. However, with our heads stuck in the cultural sand of relative truth, we think of ourselves as smart and open-minded. This delusion that contributes to a failure to pursue an examined life could prove fatal.

In this chapter, we look at truth in terms of the context of a "world-view." Some might prefer the popular and post-modern term "meta-narrative." A world-view or meta-narrative speaks of a comprehensive account of everything. It provides the big picture as it integrates all that we believe and do. It gives unity to the diversity of parts in all our lives. It contains the whole truth that a person has discovered about life and God.

A world-view ought to govern all that we believe. It provides a bird's eye view of our lives as we struggle through our daily worm's eye grind of life. It also acts as a pair of glasses through which we interpret what we see. Such glasses should be formed by the truth that we have discovered, tested and validated. A false world-view provides smudged or distorted lenses that keep a person from seeing life truly.

How do we discover and validate a true world-view?

It used to be that only those in America could be so committed to fast food. That no longer holds true today as many nations now have their share of fast food in hamburgers, tacos, wraps and chicken. This going out and getting food instead of fixing it at home supposedly lifts the burden from the one who cooks at home. In a recent commercial, one American fast food chain argued artfully in their ads that everyone would love mom if she brings home a bucket of chicken that has three different choices for the family members.

This tiny example illustrates how so many look at truth. In terms of chicken, some like it crispy; some like it hot and some like it the original recipe way. Everyone has his needs met according to personal desires and no one offends another. All choices have equal value and everyone tolerates the others' choices. Like Mama Cass in singing those lyrics, everyone sings his own song even if others sing another one or sing in a different key.

Many people say that culture and/or family acts as the critical factor in your adoption of a world-view. A Hindu, a Muslim, a Jew, or a Christian all hold on to their view of truth especially about an eternal existence because parents held a certain truth or belief. The same could be argued for an atheist or an agnostic. This argument suggests a passive adoption of a world-view because you did not choose your birthplace, parents' beliefs, culture or heritage.

Others adopt a more active yet dangerous basis for truth or world-view. People decide truth in the same way that they choose the chicken from the bucket. You pick out what fits your perceived needs or your independently chosen life-style. Everyone can have personally designed views of reality. Although your view may contradict others' views, you insure that your "my-view" still permits you to be tolerant of others' "my-view."

Another bumper sticker best expresses this approach. The bumper sticker appears in varied forms and spells out the word "Coexist." Each letter or symbol represents a different world-view. The letter "C" with a star in the middle represents the world religion of Islam. The 1960's era peace symbol forms the letter "O." This so-called peace symbol finds its origin with Nero who crucified Peter, the apostle of Jesus, upside down on a cross. The letter "e" represents science or genders. The Star of David stands for the letter "X" and represents the world religion of Judaism. Some say that the letter "I" represents the Wiccan belief or the karma wheel of Hinduism. The symbol for the conflicting forces in Chinese philosophy or Buddhism "yin and yang" stands for the letter "S." The last letter "T" represents the cross of Christianity.

Occasionally another bumper sticker uses symbols like these to spell out the word "Tolerance" with the words "believe in it" alongside the symbols. Apparently the creator of the sticker had a difficult time in finding a letter to represent atheism. Maybe just a blank would be assumed at the end of the word.

People rather commonly applaud the idea of respect for others' religions and argue for religious tolerance. A simple investigation of these religious world-views as represented by these symbols reveals ideas from each that conflict with the others. In terms of tolerant ideas co-existence cannot be possible. Every world religion has tenets that consider their own religion exclusive of any other.

The bumper sticker argues that we all ought to get along by accepting everyone's "my-truth" while we have our own "my-truth." We certainly ought to respect fellow humans but the search for a true world-view ought to transcend and take precedence over the silly notion of not wanting to offend others. What we discover as the truth may collide with what others have discovered as the truth. In terms of the "Coexist" bumper sticker, could the world-views that the symbols represent all be true? Or, are they all false? How do we validate a world-view? This leads us to some statements about how we think.

How does logic help us determine a world-view?

Philosophers have described how we think in terms of laws. These laws of logic reflect how life works and prove helpful in testing the validity of our world-view. In terms of our discussion of a world-view, one law takes precedence: the *Law of Non-contradiction.* It goes like this. The object or idea represented by "A" cannot also be the object "non-A." In other words, an object cannot be the opposite of itself. In terms of a formula it looks like this: A ≠ non-A. An apple cannot also be a non-apple. A fish cannot also be a bird or a snake or anything other than a fish at the same time.

Furthermore, in terms of ideas, two statements that oppose each other cannot both be true. Antithetical or contradictory statements cannot both be true in the same sense at the same time. For example, if a person is married (A), then that person cannot also be unmarried (non-A). If a woman is pregnant (A), then she is not at the same time not pregnant (non-A). Of course, a married person could act unmarried and a pregnant woman could hide her pregnancy. But, that does not change the facts.

Two other laws complement this one: the *Law of Identity* and the *Law of the Excluded Middle.* Daily we must exercise the Law of Identity without even thinking about the law. The law states: A thing or idea is what it claims to be. For example, if a builder goes to a local large box store to purchase a box of ¾ inch screws, he does not expect to find ½ inch screws in the box. If he does, he will discard them and maybe even be angry. As to the married person, he is a married person not an unmarried person. The pregnant woman is a pregnant woman. This may sound rudimentary and obvious but we operate like this every day. A new idiom has even appeared in our culture that reflects this idea. When things cannot be changed or you give up hope because they cannot be changed, you say, "It is what it is."

The law of the *excluded middle* prevents a choice for a middle ground when no middle option exists. If we use our previous examples, a pregnant woman cannot be something in between pregnant and not pregnant. A married man cannot have a middle position of being married and being unmarried. On the other hand, I overheard a mother say, "I have one and a half daughters-in-law." Upon further query, she referred to the engaged fiancée of her son as the half daughter in-law. She had not walked the aisle yet but the future mother-in-law anticipated that she would. In these examples a middle position or another option is excluded, eliminated or fails to make sense. You have a clear decision where no middle option exists. When no third option or middle option exists, then it cannot be chosen and is therefore excluded. You then have a true binary choice where you can choose only A or non-A.

Many of us regularly, however, commit the fallacy of the excluded middle. We do this when we set up two opposing choices as if no middle or third option truly offers itself. Someone could say, "You can only vote for either the Democratic candidate or the Republican candidate." You could choose not to vote. You might even be able to write in a candidate's name. We could also call this a false binary choice because more than just the two choices are available.

When it comes to a world-view, people seem to want a middle ground. They want a world-view that permits them to hold to views that contradict one another. They fail to see that as a logical impossibility. For example, a member of a Jewish temple might have friends who belong to an Episcopal church. In the workplace they may associate with those who practice Buddhism or even Islam. In terms of human relationships, nothing keeps these workmates from being friends, respecting each other as fellow human beings in the journey of life and enjoying their company.

The problem does not lie in their acceptance of each other but rather in their acceptance of each other's world-view as the same. Although each world-view has exclusive statements that oppose each other, these four friends may seek the excluded middle ground by holding the view that all religions are the same and that all these religions or world-views equally have the truth about life and God. On the other hand, each one could be a "cultural" believer. In other words, they only take casually the moniker of Muslim, Jew, Hindu or Christian; they really do not care to know what their "birth" religion teaches.

What questions enable the discovery of a valid world-view?

What questions must be satisfied in our discovery of a world-view? The laws of logic mentioned above and the questions below give us some guidelines and method in validating reasonably and straightforwardly the world-views so that we can live confidently with our choice.

1. **Question of Undeniability**: Can my discovery be denied? Take the statement: All Pacific Islanders come from Fiji. A quick glance at a globe shows other nations in the Pacific such as Tonga or Polynesia. These parts disprove the truth of the statement. It can now be denied and proven false.

2. **Question of Consistency:** Does my discovery best fit life as it really is? Does it answer the laws of logic so that it makes sense?

3. **Question of Evil:** Does my discovery resolve my shortcomings, explain the shortcomings of others and account for suffering in the world?

4. **Question of Hope:** Does my discovery really work on a daily basis and give genuine encouragement and freedom to look forward to the future?

Does "my" world-view—"my truth"—do justice to these questions? Does "my" world-view best answer these questions? Can I with confidence live out "my" world-view? Does "my" world-view provide the worth to the works that I need to do? The pursuit of truth, especially what leads to worth, means that a person who seeks the truth must answer the above questions and use the laws of logic to validate the knowledge that he discovers as the truth.

Can we avoid the truth if we deny it?

Truth has a troubling aspect for all of us if we choose to chase it down: it cannot be denied no matter your denial of it. Truth does not change because of time, culture, place or people. If Neil Armstrong walked on the moon in July, 1969, that fact remains true today no matter where you live, no matter the language that you speak and no matter the nation where you live. [Some conspiracy theorists still deny the reasonable evidence and contend that the federal government hoodwinked us and no one ever went to the moon.] Truth also has an absolute nature to it. Relative truth would prove contradictory and could be life-threatening.

If you discover two contradictory statements, then the choices seem obvious in terms of reasoning. One must be true; one must be false or both could be false. Both cannot be true. This makes truth and, in turn, a world-view non-contradictory in its internal characteristics. To develop and validate a world-view does not require one to know everything but what we know and believe must be reasonable. We live by what we believe whether we have adopted a world-view passively via upbringing or actively by considering and validating other truth options.

A world-view could also be difficult to accept as a lifestyle because adopting a new world-view means change. This does mean that what we discover could make us uncomfortable. What we discover might upset us in the good sense because we would have to change for the better. After all, who wants to have a view and not also live out that view? We could find seeming contradictions that gain resolution as we explore more of our new world-view.

Who can escape a world-view?

This chapter spoke of a world-view as that grand narrative about life and God that would explain the diversity of the parts where we live and move. It spoke about the nature of truth, statements of truth and how to validate a world-view. Fundamentally, truth has an absolute, undeniable and exclusive nature. Our laws of logic support those characteristics of truth. If I state that all baseball fans love the Yankees, then the production of a baseball fan who loved the Dodgers would disprove that idea.

In our daily lives, we live by the laws of logic and by the questions that lead us to the truth about anything. We want the physician to tell us if we have cancer or not. If he does find cancer, we want to know so that we can deal with it. We all know the feeling personally or vicariously from others about being in that middle ground where we wait for the cancer report to return. That middle ground produces anxiety and hopelessness. We want to be on the side of the truth when it comes to everyday living. We want to know, "Do we have cancer or do we not have cancer?" We all remain uncomfortable in the middle ground where we cannot know. In life-threatening moments, honesty rules even if in other venues theologians, philosophers or politicians do not live in reality. In regard to life, a commentator has proclaimed simply, "I live in Realville…" And so must we.

No one lives without a world-view. Like Pilate, we may want to avoid an answer to the question: "What is truth?" We could avoid discovery of a world-view because that discovery could force us to change. We might have to surrender something that we love. We might have to break relationships because of differences with our friends and family over our newly found conclusions. But, without the truth about anything and especially without the truth about a world-view, how do you know who you are and how do you know what to do?

Unfortunately, we now live in a culture that wants to believe that contradictory ideas may both be true. The law of non-contradiction has fallen out of fashion today. It looks antiquated and unacceptable in a world of accommodation and political correctness. However, truth and contradiction prove to be miserable bed fellows. Something cannot be both true and false at the same time. Today, many of us also choose not to think and consider *People* magazine and its numerous grocery store tabloid rack cousins as our literary fare. There we find the influential people of the pop culture who may gain respect for their glamour but lack respect for their usually inane and contradictory views.

In spite of the previous explanations about how we must live logically, many of us tend to live in what cultural observers or philosophers have called a two-story framework. In the lower story sits verifiable ideas; the upper story contains unverifiable ideas. The lower story deals with everyday living and things that we all accept as the truth in order to traverse our daily living. The upper story deals with the truth about the overall narrative of life. That would include discussions about morality or the existence of God or angels or even demons.

Many consider ideas in the upper story as unverifiable, open to a variety of acceptable conclusions and therefore not worthy of much discussion. Such discussions used to take place on the campuses of our universities. More importantly, many feel uncomfortable in bringing these ideas up among friends. Such upper-story opinions must remain in the private and personal arena or be confined in the cloistered arena of temples, churches or mosques. Too many of us choose not to deal with the upper story and the culture has supported us in this by removing religion, values and morality from the public square.

To neglect reasoning where choices have their shaking-out could prove lethal both now and later.

You could live like what Mama Cass sang. You will have your own individual view even if no one will sing along because they cannot understand the reasoning and the validity of your world-view or because, by accepting your world-view, you will accept theirs even if both lack logic or validity.

Part Two: Worth Pursuing *A Proposal*

John Saxe penned the poem "The Six Men of Indostan." Six blind men examined an elephant with their hands. Each had confidence about what he felt but erroneously concluded what the part revealed about the animal that they felt. To the observer who had the whole picture because he had eyes to see, he rightly concludes that they had all examined a part of an elephant. Only the person who could see it all could determine the overall picture clearly.

> *"And so these men of Indostan disputed loud and long,*
> *Each in his own opinion exceeding stiff and strong;*

Though each was partly in the right; all were in the wrong."

We live somewhat like the blind men in that we cannot know all the details or parts when it comes to determining a world-view. We must make a conclusion about a world-view according to the parts that we discover. The discovery of the parts calls us to make a conclusion about those parts. As finite beings we have no other option but to make conclusions on what has been revealed to us. As small creatures in a vast universe we cannot know exhaustively but we can know truly. What we know truly can give us meaning to all that we will or can know.

The following chapter will discuss a part [trait or detail] that every world-view must touch and attempt to explain. After this next chapter the one after that will address one specific world-view. You may think that you know that one specific world-view; but, as an adage says, familiarity breeds contempt. But, ignorance cannot be bliss.

6

The Undeniability of Death: Who Can Escape Death?

"As an unbelieving fatalist, I can only sink into a state of resignation when faced with the horror of death."

Sigmund Freud, father of psychoanalysis

Lynn Hill won thirty international rock climbing titles. Before she ascended one day in May of 1989, she stopped in the midst of her protocol to tie her shoes. Although something seemed undone to her, she ascended. When she reached the ascent of her climb, she leaned back to repel and fell downward seventy-two feet. Tree branches broke her fall so that she escaped serious injury or death. She had disregarded her misgivings because she abided by her OHIO protocol of "Only Handle It Once." She had become so familiar or automatic with her routine that when she failed to attach the safety rope, she did not notice it. On this occasion she had, as the idiom says, "cheated death."

Pat Tillman won his fame as an undersized, hard-hitting safety that played for Arizona State and then the Arizona Cardinals. Those who knew him would have considered him tough on the outside and tender on the inside. He had at least two notable and outstanding character traits. He had a desire to protect the little guy and he had a passion to live without regard to risk. To once help his undersized friend after an attack, he mistakenly beat up an innocent person and eventually served a month in lock-up and in community service to pay for his crime. In the off-season of the NFL, he would run a marathon or compete as a triathlete. He would risk a leap off a cliff to dive into unexplored water below. Such feats energized him but could have jeopardized his NFL career.

Both these passions to protect and to risk came together one early evening in an Afghanistan creek bed. Although he would give up a million dollar NFL contract he enlisted along with his brother to endure the rigors of gaining the status of a Ranger in the U.S. Army after the 9/11 attack on America. On a patrol on April 22, 2004, Tillman ran back into a canyon in Afghanistan and in spite of pounds of equipment, he climbed rapidly up its side to aid his brother whom he thought had entered an ambush. That evening this robust, healthy, young man would die and his fame would grow nationally first as an assumed hero whose enemies had killed him and then as a victim of fratricide as the truth finally came out that his confused comrades had inadvertently taken his life. The passionate, unselfish, strong and risk-taking Tillman would not escape death that time.

In spite of the inevitability of death, many pretend that death will not come. They refuse to make out a Last Will and Testament or to prepare their financial and personal papers for others. Many refuse to see the end of life even as others around them take their final breath. After they gather with the living to honor the death of a friend, the thoughts of death they still deny. Unfortunately, like the climber Lynn Hill, we have become so occupied with daily routines or living on cruise control that we cannot contemplate the morbid thought of death. Like those who loved and/or respected Pat Tillman, they cannot fathom the demise of such a one. They may think like we all do about our departed friends, "He is gone away temporarily and will someday walk back into our lives again."

Others attempt to escape death by denying it. Robert Craig "Evel" Knievel, daredevil and entertainer, thrilled thousands in the 1970's by death-defying leaps over automobiles and even a canyon. While he held the record at one point of the most broken bones of a living person according to *Guinness* at 433, Evel did not succumb to a motorcycle crash on a casino parking lot or destruction on a canyon wall but rather in a bed from pulmonary fibrosis. Public glory had escaped him and he would also not escape death.

In a less dramatic but also in a rationalistic way, the rest of us deny death. We refuse to go to funerals or contract an agent of life and/or health insurance. On a religious level, others even practice some sort of belief system that sees death as an illusion and sometimes even life as a dream. Our experience seems to refute that we live in a dream. We see our friends or family members cosmetically prepared and displayed before us without breath and life and want to believe this macabre display cannot be happening. We may even linger as others will lower the corrupted flesh of our loved ones into the ground.

We have so naturally occupied ourselves with daily living that we fail to contemplate the morbid thought of eternal dying. We may escape death temporarily and not die on the ground at the bottom of a rock wall. We may take leaps on overpowered wheeled machines and dare death to take us. We may volunteer for combat and assume that the other guy will die.

However, this awful slayer follows every one of us. We cannot elude this unrelenting pursuer who abruptly interrupts the life-giving rhythm of our hearts and who stains the faces of our family with the tears of grief. Most of us will not even consider slightly this grave consequence or consider an escape from it. We cannot overcome this undeterred stalker who steals our breath and delivers our demise. While death chases us, the desire to live resides strongly within us and we act as if we will live forever. In an ironic tragedy we know that we will die but we live as if we will not.

No one can deny the fact of mortality but we cannot think of our own death. We do not mind death; we just do not want to be around when it comes. To understand or achieve true worth, we must begin to think about and discuss honestly and open mindedly the truth about death since the possession of worth and true hope reside in a resolution of death.

Why won't we consider this issue of death?

"It is better to debate a question before settling it than to settle a question before debating it."

An old adage

For a few years, I worked for an organization whose leaders would conduct free-wheeling large discussion groups in homes with the promised topic of "Life and God." We would always begin with three promises: "this will last exactly 59 minutes and 50 seconds; this will be a discussion and not a lecture and we will have a Bible that only the leader can consult if someone wants the Bible's answer to a question." Rarely, if ever, did that Bible open because the different views on any topic in a skeptical venue took up the whole 59 minutes and 50 seconds.

As the weekly series stretched out for the whole month, different participants began to dominate and to defend publicly and sometimes boldly their view of life and God. Each of these advocates began to practice an "apologetic" for his or her set of beliefs. While an apology means a public regret about wrongs toward another, an apologetic means a defense for what you believe to be true. Before you can defend to others what you believe, you have to prove first to yourself what you believe and why you believe the way that you do. The most skeptical among us may be those who can best explain their beliefs because they have thoroughly tested them. Doubt polishes our set of beliefs so that it shines even more brightly and clearly to us.

Many of us avoid any sort of apologetic about what we believe in the arena of God, life and death because a settled set of beliefs can produce conflict not just within ourselves but with others around us. For example, in these discussions where a variety of religious views proliferated, predictable common arguments came up in a heated emotional fashion either during the discussion or during the dessert time later.

One argument would go something like this, "You are a Christian because you grew up in a Christian home. If you had grown up in Asia, you would probably be a Buddhist or a Muslim or Hindu. After all, millions practice Islam and other beliefs because their parents practiced it." In the group setting, many participants would find it unkind to dismiss such unproven and strongly held conclusions and would quietly permit them without opposition. So the thinking goes, "We must be polite and not offend even if the speaker lacks logic or truth."

Another argument came from one elderly Jewish man who later said to me, "I would never quit Judaism because of my dear mother who kept me alive during the Great Depression by picking up fallen coal on the train tracks to heat our house. I owe it to her." Such arguments prove emotionally comforting to the holder of the view but difficult to oppose by the listener.

Questioning another's experience and the interpretation of that experience could sound like a character attack to the speaker. To attempt to refute others with such emotionally bound conclusions may lead to a break in the relationship with that person.

In spite of possible conflict with others, to know what you know and how you came to know does matter because what you know can affect how you live. What you refuse to know could kill you. A dose of medicine cannot be the same as an overdose of medicine. If you thought that anti-inflammatory tablets could cure you, you might fail to see a physician for your orthopedic injury. As a side note, America spends millions upon millions of dollars to research and solve endemic medical problems such as diabetes, cancer, AIDs and even the common cold. Who has not given at some point money to national organizations that commit themselves to solving such diseases? We accept the truth that children and others can escape these kinds of illnesses if we just give enough money because money will create hard-working, bright researchers.

Yet, on a personal level where we live and die, we choose to act and live as if we can prevent death altogether. Or, we smugly put it so far out into the future that we do not have to think about its arrival. While we may give money to solve illnesses that lead to death, we refuse to give thoughts about the cause of our own death. We read the obituaries of others almost dispassionately but never consider that someday others will read our obituary.

The truth about life beyond the grave can frame our lives so that we face death straightforwardly and live now quite fully. We fail to seek out the truth because the results of such search can turn our lives and the lives of our friends and family upside down. We find it painful to upset our emotionally comfortable status since dramatic change could cause even our closest friends to see our views as threatening or antagonistic to them. We may lose friends because they no longer want to be around someone who lacks an "open mind." Thus, we cannot think about death and its cause. We may fear loss of a friendship and family more than we fear loss of our lives because we choose not to discover the truth, especially about death.

In short, we choose to "feel" our way through life and not "think" about meaning, purpose, or significance. The prospect of death ought to make us think and not just feel.

Without a true narrative about this issue of separation that we call death, we cannot know what really matters; we fail to find comfort when what matters to us fades away and we cannot live as we ought.

Even daily living could eventually be unrewarding.

What do we say about death?

"Death has this much to be said for it. You don't have to get out of bed for it. Wherever you happened to be, they bring it to you—free."
KINGSLEY AMIS, NOTED LATE BRITISH AUTHOR

Most cultures throughout history have burial rituals that assume some kind of life after death. The ancient Chinese would bury their rulers with items like pillows that would make their afterlife more comfortable. Many of us have seen pictures of the burial plot of Qin Shin Huang, the first emperor of China, whose followers had interned him with terra-cotta warriors and horses to accompany him into the afterlife. Some indigenous peoples of the Americas would bury their loved ones with objects to be used in the next life. The Vikings left burial items according to the social status that the deceased had in this life to ensure the same status in the next life. In past Hindu cultures, if the husband died, the widow would be burned with the deceased husband to be with him.

Ancient Judaism looked forward to a future of resurrection of the dead as the prophet Daniel spoke, "And many of them that sleep in the dust of the earth shall awake, some to everlasting life, and some to shame *and* everlasting contempt." (Daniel 12.2)

While Buddhists would argue that the immaterial part of man returns to some sort of "mind stream," they would also see something in existence beyond the grave. Through the life and death cycle of birth and re-birth their hope lies in finally escaping into Nirvana. No one knows much about this location or existence because the Buddha described it as "incomprehensible, indescribable, inconceivable, unutterable…"

Hindus with their many gods would argue for a transmigration of souls who inhabit future bodies of animals or humans depending on their works in a past life. Their view denies the uniqueness of each person. They would also say that maybe eventually, the soul could escape this cyclical bondage of reincarnation and return to some sort of eternal state.

As an exception, atheists might argue that death has no door to open after life.

In short, except for atheists, most cultures in every place would present a world-view that sees something after death.

At its core, religion ought to do at least three things: *resolve suffering* and its accompanying fear now and later; *give the hope* of an enduring, fruitful life now and later; and *provide the ability to live with purpose* in life now and later.

Every religion has to deal with suffering and its accompanying ultimate evil of death. Buddhism even recognizes that "to live is to suffer." Additionally, virtually every culture attempts to resolve the fear that death puts into the human heart. This applies whether some indigenous dweller in the darkest part of a tropical rain forest sacrifices animals to appease the spirits or the ardent elderly widow who continues to light the numerous candles every morning in the cathedral for her deceased loved ones.

This attention to an afterlife suggests that most of us think that death cannot have the last word. Who of us fails to have a sense of some sort of eternity? The cause of death that appears in autopsies and death certificates really enumerates secondary issues such as diseases, accidents or crime. When a very elderly person dies, the death certificate lists the cause of death as "natural causes" if no other known immediate cause presents itself.

With blank looks and wet eyes, we stare downward toward a golden or copper clad box where the mortal remains of our loved ones lay and we don't want to consider this moment as natural. We blunt our grief with well-intended but trite phrases like "he had a good life" or "she lived a full life." Worst yet, in our awkwardness about grief, we may hurtfully blurt out, "he just looks like he is asleep." In the case of the death of the so-called innocent —the young and/or the beautiful—we don't hesitate to question death as anything but "natural."

However, from one theological point of view, everyone who dies—young and old alike—dies of a natural cause. We all die naturally because the seed of death rests in our own very nature. Only in that sense does death come naturally and it does not mean the absolute end of one's existence.

Why does anyone have to die?

In 1908, *The Times* newspaper of London asked several British writers and leading intellectuals to respond to the question, "What's wrong with the world?" G. K. Chesterton, the esteemed Catholic journalist and "prince of paradox" as a writer, responded with one post card. He had written on it this succinct message, "Dear Sirs, I am. Sincerely yours, G. K. Chesterton."

Not quite a century beyond Chesterton, Karl Menninger wrote in 1973 the book *Whatever Became of Sin?* He argued that sin as a concept of moral wrong or human misbehavior had disappeared from everyday life. He regretted that loss since he saw sin as something that hurts others or does harm to our fellow human beings and we must speak about it in that way. Robert Schuller, retired televangelist and founder of the now bankrupt mega-church Crystal Cathedral in Garden Grove, California says this about sin, "Sin is any act or thought that robs me or another human being of his or her self-esteem."

David Gelernter in his book *Drawing Life: Surviving the Unabomber* matter-of-factly begins his book with this sentence, "One morning in June 1993 I was almost killed by a mail bomb." The so-called Unabomber chose this gifted writer and professor of programming to be destroyed. Gelernter then proposes the theme of his story, "… it's much harder to put things back together than to smash them up." As we will eventually see, the requirement to put things back together in the eternal venue also proves to be difficult and extraordinary but not impossible.

As Chesterton noted, a look in the mirror reveals the cause for problems in the world. A positive thinker like Robert Schuller or a trained physician like Menninger rightly confirm that sin does exist and that it does harm others although they do not see it as that bad. In many instances, a person like David Galernter refuses to let the sin of another curtail his ability to succeed.

Few of us have broken societal laws so much that it justified judicial proceedings and imprisonment. Few of us have done anything as evil as the deeds of the Unabomber. Whatever label we may want to give to our imperfections—sin, lawlessness or missing the mark —, no one can deny the quip that Chesterton writes. We have fallen short and bear responsibility for our own problems and for conflicts that we cause to others.

Just as we cannot deny the inevitability of death, we cannot deny ourselves as its cause.

Sin causes death and it lies at the bottom of every problem and produces conflict with awful effects. Conflict undermines and even dissolves friendship. Everyone has experienced the thorny and poisonous fruit that conflict bears. Unresolved conflict yields a harvest of hurt feelings, lengthy silence, purposed avoidance, devalued relationship and even sometimes passive retribution.

To revive or resurrect the friendship, the offending party must apologize and maybe even offer compensation for restitution. More than flowers may have to accompany the apology. The offending party must change. The one who delivered the punch of temporary dissolution usually must pursue the wronged party and be reconciled.

Reconciliation describes the act of renewing the torn relationship. Over time, without any desire to reconcile, the relationship loses all worth. Those who cannot reconcile with one another cannot be friends and can, in time, act as enemies because estrangement can multiply enmity.

Why does estrangement bring death?

A Christian world-view argues that the harmful actions that we do to others with regard to estrangement reveals a dark side of the human condition. In spite of this awful harm to fellow humans on this horizontal plane, this harm shrinks in comparison to the harm that has resulted in a divine estrangement on the vertical plane.

Man's standing and man's actions put him in conflict with God and therefore estranged from Him. Both the nature of man and the deeds of man confirm the veracity of this Heavenly indictment of man's rebellion. That indictment prevents communion between the unholy, corrupted creature and the holy, incorruptible Creator. No one of earth escapes this indictment. In both nature and behavior, we continue to oppose God. We want our own way. We cannot be reconciled until we accept the cause of our estrangement.

The Christian world-view places Adam, the first man as innocent and untested and living in a perfect environment where he could obey; worship and serve God, His Creator. He could count God as his friend. God had created man in His image. That image would include spiritual access to God; emotions to respond to God and to fellow humans; intellect to understand choices; a determining will to execute choices; creativity to express; conscience to be moral or just; and an unconfirmed holiness.

When God created Adam, he expected him to prove his love through obedience to His desires and to the stewardship of purpose that God had given him. He had unconfirmed or untested loyalty. Adam eventually refused to be loyal, intentionally disobeyed and suffered the judgment of expulsion from the Garden and the judgment of eventual physical death. Since that moment which takes the label of "the Fall" or "the original sin," all of us who dwell on earth inherit a will that opposes God and inherit a judgment that includes death.

In belief and in practice, we live estranged as His enemies because in our nature and in our actions we lack holiness.

In this Heavenly discord, man has wronged God not just by acts of intentional disobedience but by his state of unrighteousness. Even the youngest or the best among us cannot attain to His holiness let alone live out a perfect life.

Who made Adam my representative?

You may object to your condemnation because of a choice made long ago by one man. This objection falls under the old adage of "Life is not fair!" You could make a list of those issues in life where you had no opportunity to choose.

The most obvious illustration comes in the parents that you had and all the upstream genes that you inherited. You may change the color of your hair or make your body more powerful or employ a surgeon to give you a different nose. Nonetheless, a lot of what you have you had no choice in the matter. Many folks such as athletes or artists or investors who succeed don't mind the genes that they have inherited. This does not imply that genes determine the whole future of any of us.

In the realm of externals, many laws and traditions that determine your way of life you had no part in their formation. On the other hand, you may enjoy freedoms and privileges that came from the suffering of those who preceded you. We cannot deny certain physical boundaries such as gravity. We also cannot deny the existence of spiritual boundaries or sin in our lives no matter the name that we give to it and no matter our unsupported denial that Adam has no part in us.

As the historian Garry Wills has said, humankind "has a past." He refers to a past of evil that man has committed. Historic or Biblical Christianity argues that what we have we have not always had. We have not always been this way. Alien evil invaded our existence. That choice came when that one man Adam chose for us. We must resist the urge to say, "I did not vote for him to represent me." The opposing argument would say, "You would have done the same."

The CBS show *60 Minutes* aired a program on February 6, 1983 where the late Mike Wallace interviewed Yehiel Dinur, a survivor of Auschwitz. To set up the interview, Wallace ran a video clip of the moment when Mr. Dinur walked into the courtroom in June, 1961 to testify against Adolph Eichmann. Eichmann had executed millions of

Jews and others as the premier overseer in what he and the other Nazis would call "The Final Solution." The Israeli court declared that for Eichmann "the particulars of his rank and function did not excuse his actions." In the clip, Mr. Dinur came into the courtroom and stopped when he saw Eichmann, the one who had authorized his internment in the concentration camp. He began to sob and then collapse as others came to carry him out.

After the clip ran, the energetic and prurient Wallace had to ask, "*How is it possible for a man to act as Eichmann acted? Was he a monster? A madman? Or was he perhaps something even more terrifying: was he normal*?" The former prisoner, after forty some years of freedom could answer in the negative, 'No.' He attributed his breakdown in the courtroom to two observations. Neither fantastic observation ought to surprise honest people. First, he had recognized Eichmann as no extraordinary monster but just an ordinary man like himself. Second, he saw Eichmann in himself as he candidly stated, "*I was afraid about myself. I saw that I am capable to do this. I am… exactly like he [is] …* ***Eichmann is in all of us…***'

7

Gaining Worth by Overcoming Death

"It is easier to denature plutonium than to denature the evil spirit of men."

Albert Einstein

Thirty-five years ago my good friend who had done very well in business moved to the nation's capital where he thought that he would make even more money by developing a larger network of contacts. He attended a party one night where many young Congressional staffers worked. My winsome and unassuming friend extended his hand toward another guest at the party as he intended to introduce himself with a mannerly greeting and his name. The stranger did not give his hand or his name and matter-of-factly greeted him by saying, "I am on the staff of Congressman [Name withheld]." This ugly and endemic attitude of unveiled elevation above others as empowered by unrestrained selfish ambition takes the wide road away from the worth added life.

Genuine worth has no place for human pride.

To the detriment of our culture, those in Washington, D.C. have no monopoly on missing opportunities for friendship by putting others that they meet on unequal footing with them by acting in a condescending or patronizing way. Friendship begins when the parties to the friendship can meet on an equal footing without regard to any sort of disparity such as education, wealth, age, possessions or position. True friendship thrives when parties reconcile by resolving what disparities keep the friends apart.

These hurdles of disparity and the lack of reconciliation also hold true on the vertical plane to enter into a friendship with God. Concerning the disparity of status, no unrighteous person has equal footing with a righteous God. Concerning the disparity of behavior, a lawless creature cannot have a relationship with the eternal Law Giver. Concerning the disparity of being, the finite cannot know the Infinite without His choice to permit friendship with Him.

Without a resolution of these disparities, man has no friendship with God. Worst yet, God considers man His enemy. Man's present natural willfulness and unrighteousness continue to alienate himself from the Creator. On the horizontal level, that alienation also proves to be the source of our alienation from one another. Man must change but change eludes him. How can God disregard these disparities?

A Christian world-view does not leave us stuck with just the description of man's problem—namely: man fails in his ability to please God or to satisfy His demands of holiness.

A Christian world-view explains the source of separation from God and offers a solution to this disparity between a holy God and unholy man.

Most importantly, a Christian world-view also presents a solution to death that results in a multiplied worth to man now, explains purpose in this life now and provides a certain hope of a future or eternal life later.

In our nation's capital success may not depend upon the truth of your good ideas but on whom you know. In terms of a Christian world-view, success and satisfaction in life and recovery from death depends both upon a choice to accept truth and upon the One who revealed it to you. Friendship with God grants true worth and worth like no other worth.

How does God set aside His divine status and resolve conflict in order to have friendship with His creatures?

Why does the work of man fail to provide a means to worth?

Before we see how a Christian world-view resolves human failure and gives man worth, let's consider an alternative from a rabbi whose comments ran in a newspaper on Yom Kippur, the Day of Atonement, the holiest day of the Jewish year. While his comments come from his view of Judaism, his words speak for many of all kinds of religious persuasions about how to overcome this separation between God and man.

This rabbi has commented that "Judaism is not the only religion that teaches that we human beings are flawed, that we are often careless and impulsive." With that statement a Christian world-view would agree with the rabbi. We live and walk as flawed men and women although flawed could suggest acceptable weakness and not offensive to God or unholy.

He continues as he contrasts other faiths with Judaism with these comments, "It is not our *admission* of sinfulness, but our *definition* of it. For some faiths … 'sinful' is something you are, not something you do. Viewed this way, human nature is inherently flawed." He continues, "Judaism teaches something entirely different. Judaism teaches that 'sinful' is not what you are, but what you do."

A Christian world-view parts company with the rabbi because a Christian world-view sees man as condemned due to his nature as a sinner as well as his actions of sin. His fallen nature and his flawed actions separate man from God. Man fails to do what he must do to please God.

The rabbi proposes his appealing and supposedly workable solution for mankind. "We have sinned, we have transgressed, but we can also soothe and heal the wounds we have inflicted. We can begin again if we are willing to look in the mirror and make a change by matching our promises with our own performance. Each of us alone must decide to be better or worse. Each of us must decide to do better or worse than we've ever done before. That choice isn't God's, it's ours."

These statements naturally bring up some questions. Can flawed man make a choice to break with his past and decide to begin to please God? Can we, without help, match "our promises with our performances?" Can we on our own resolve disparity between us and God?

The idea of "flawed" behavior blunts the definition of sin. The word "flawed" suggests imperfect but acceptable. It suggests imperfect but able to be overlooked. For example, shoppers look for the bargains and may travel miles to get them at the outlet mall. This fairly recent retail idea helps the manufacturer by profitably disposing of flawed, rejected or overrun goods. It helps the frugal shopper who accepts the flawed items because they consider the flaws insignificant and/or easily hidden. Our disparities do not take the label of insignificant so as not to be noticed or even so insignificant that they can be overlooked by God.

People find the rabbi's arguments very appealing. The rabbi's "flawed" man has such small flaws that man himself can solve them through a commitment to change. His "flawed" man can by himself decide to do better and to please God. In short, "I am not that bad and I can change if I want to change."

The late Senator Patrick Moynihan coined the phrase "defining deviancy down." Moynihan argued that in the last half century Americans have lowered the threshold of acceptable behavior. On Valentine's Day in 1927, as he alludes, Americans labeled the murder of seven men by five gangsters a massacre. We now find ourselves inundated and yet seemingly unconcerned and unaffected by the regularity of reported multiple murders throughout the whole of the country. Newspapers have always profited on the motto, "Bad news leads." As they say in media about getting the viewers' attention, "If it bleeds, it leads."

Our self-delusion causes us to argue that we can change so that God finds us acceptable. We even convince ourselves that the desire or intention to change ranks on the same level as change itself. This common thinking about change lacks success both in theory and in practice. How many times have any of us tried to change or please others and failed miserably?

We also all know in our experience the difficulty of change. Thousands earn a living on helping people to change yet even prescription drugs may fail them. Even if we could change, could we change enough to reconcile an unholy man with a holy God and then please Him by our actions?

A Christian world-view parts radically with the comments of the rabbi and the comments of all other alternatives that "dumbs down" sin or keeps sin from discarding its rightful label of "bad news." When it comes to the character of man in respect to the demands of God, "flawed" does not fit the description of man at all from God's perspective. He sees man's flaws as significant. When it comes to sin, the culture has dubbed behavior that would offend God as acceptable to society.

What society used to call weird, unnatural or unlawful now carries the label of permissible, possibly lawful and maybe even respected. If we accept such unlawfulness at the larger cultural level, why would we condemn ourselves at our own smaller private level?

No one should wonder why so many folks regardless of religious persuasion or lack thereof would readily side with the rabbi. They would argue in voice and attempt in lifestyle to make up for past deeds and, as a result, please

God. Self-delusion permits us to consider ourselves as not that bad. We lessen the gravity of our sins and evade responsibility for them because we have devalued the seriousness of the worst kinds of societal behavior.

We fail to see that the flawed fruit that we have borne and do bear reveals a fallen and rebellious person who cannot change enough to please God and therefore continues to stand guilty before the Almighty Judge. We may agree with the late Senator that our society has lowered greatly moral standards or defined deviancy "down" to our own detriment.

God cannot define sin "down."

What other bad news does death bring?

"Everyone is entitled to his own set of opinions but not his own set of facts."

Patrick J. Moynihan

In spite of a culture that defines deviancy down, a Christian world-view argues that divine justice has not gone out of style. Lawbreakers must pay a penalty. "If you commit the crime then you must do the time." You may deny this observation because you think, "What 'time' would I do? I will die, be done with this life and no longer exist." Many think in this way but a Christian world-view would argue strongly against that. Moreover, an unrighteous person faces more than the penalty of a physical death from a righteous God.

Lawless man faces three kinds of death. Simply put, death means separation. The statistic that one out of every one of us dies speaks of the most familiar and obviously undeniable kind of separation: physical death. This death separates the material part of a person—the outer you—from the immaterial part of a person—the inner you. This death also separates the physically living from the physically dead. Those mourners who remain behind weep not just for the loss of the departed one but also for themselves since they now have demonstrable and ugly confirmation of their eventual and guaranteed terminus. These thoughts may seem macabre and even worthy of avoidance but this reality even the skeptics must consider because death will eventually not be denied.

The two other kinds of death receive little attention outside of theological venues and produce hot debates about them. The next and second kind of separation concerns spiritual death. Everyone who is born alive physically is also born dead spiritually. This paradox of being alive physically but dead spiritually accounts for our lawless behaviors. It also accounts for our inability to understand that God is there and that He has spoken.

This does not prevent even the most irreligious or atheistic among us from growing up and achieving great heights in the arts, in the sciences, in commerce, in sports, in humanitarian efforts because we carry—albeit marred—the image of God. On the other hand, we can descend great depths as we also wage lawless wars, destroy the environment and act in relationships as beasts toward one another. Although we may bear His marred image and do wonderful deeds, we yet remain estranged from Him.

The third and final kind of death concerns eternal separation. A person who dies physically and never gains a spiritual enlivening as the friend of God suffers the third kind of separation or eternal death. This eternal death keeps the spiritually and physically dead person condemned and estranged forever from God in the afterlife. This sounds so harsh and unfair that even the most conservative of theologians find such idea repugnant because it denies the idea of a God who loves His creation.

How shall we think of any proposal concerning death's cause?

We have made the following assumptions:

* *God exists as holy; we exist as unholy.*
* *We seek our own good and not the good of God.*
* *We are born into corruption.*
* *We cannot escape corruption by ourselves.*

Such defilement separates us from God because corruption cannot dwell with incorruption. Unresolved continual defilement will guarantee at death a permanently broken fellowship throughout eternity. The Creator and His creatures can only dwell together as friends and that comes according to the Creator's demands.

In His universe He demands that wrongs must eventually be righted. In the case of man, God demands physical death—separation of the immaterial from the material—as man's punishment. Unfortunately, this death fails as a payment to satisfy God for man to regain fellowship with God. Eternal estrangement follows as the eventual effect of earthly estrangement. Thus man remains eternally condemned because His justice demands nothing less.

Such severe sentence may sound primitive, barbaric, and grossly unfair. As harsh as this sentence sounds it does make sound sense if the world-view presented here is the truth about God and about man. Whatever beliefs that we hold or whatever "truths" that we have accepted, we cannot deny the fact that death does not discriminate. The grave will eventually claim each one of us: both the foolish and the wise; the unknown and the well-known; the ugly and the beautiful; the poor and the rich. One out of every one of us will die. Death proclaims that ultimately it has the final say in this life because no one can overcome it except God Himself. It so accents the ultimate human Achilles heel of weakness.

Why should we consider this proposal about death?

If you have digested the preceding argument, then you have rightly understood the essence of Christian theology in regard to the anthropology of man. You could quickly dismiss the Christian answer because of the European slaughters of the Crusades, the atrocities of the Holocaust or even the barbarism of the Spanish Inquisition because they all have in some way been erroneously characterized as the result of a Christian world-view. But, then, you would have to dismiss atheism as an answer to the issues of life because of the pogroms [government led systematic annihilation of specific groups] put forth by atheistic leaders in Russia and China.

Lenny Bruce, the obscenity-ridden comedian and certainly no advocate for a Christian world-view, said it a little differently, "People are leaving the churches in droves and returning to God." We cannot ask him what he meant but he seems to assume that the church because of its hypocrisy keeps people from God. That blame could suggest that what the visible church holds to be true lacks trustworthiness.

Orthodoxy—what you believe—ought to produce an orthopraxy—what you do. Your behavior must align itself with your belief.

Too often those who claim to know the truth fail to practice it. Mr. Bruce may have failed to embrace the truth because he failed to find faithful followers of it.

We must be careful about rejecting the truth just because those who know the truth fail to practice it as they ought. Their failure to practice the truth does not make the truth less true. Truth remains true in spite of others' disregard of it or their haphazard application of it.

John Donne, an English poet and Anglican preacher under King James I, wrote sonnets about life, love and death. Literature lovers will remember him as the one who wrote that "no man is an island." He lived in a time when the church rang its bell to signal events such as prayer times and church gatherings. The church also rang its bell for funerals. In regard to death, he wrote, "... [You should] never send [someone] to know [find out] for whom the bell tolls; it tolls for thee."

In this case, the context refers to death. Whenever we hear the bell that rings out another's death, we ought to grieve because of the departure of that person. The bell ought also to be a warning to every person about his eventual death. Donne understood the need for every person to remember that death awaits each of us eventually.

Death as a determined end may not surprise us but the date of our death will probably always surprise us. We may believe in the fact of the death of others but we refuse to believe that we will die. We don't mind death; we just don't want to be around when it comes.

Unless you suffer from some malady or addiction that distorts your view of life, you want to live. You have a conviction that you ought not to die. One day you will die and others will hear the bell that rings for you. This longing to live will give someone who intentionally chooses to die the moniker of psychopath or terrorist or even hero.

The late Christopher Hitchens, writer and avowed atheist, said it this way in an article about trite sayings on pain as he suffered awfully in dying full of pain from esophageal cancer. His quote refers to the saying attributed to Friedrich Nietzsche, "What does not kill me makes me stronger." Hitchens commented, "So far, I have decided to take whatever my disease can throw at me, and to stay combative even while taking the measure of my inevitable decline.... It is our common fate. In either case, though, one can dispense with facile maxims that don't live up to their apparent billing."

In short, this atheist whose brother holds an opposing world-view recognized the pain and inevitability of death. This common and inevitable fate awaits every one of us and we cannot deflect its power unless we know the cause for it. As Hitchens suffered he came to this inescapable and harsh truth: We will all die physically.

8

The Necessity of God's Work of Worth to Overcome Death

"The person and work of Christ is the rock upon which the Christian religion is built… take Christ from Christianity, and you disembowel it, there is practically nothing left.
Christ is the center of Christianity."

John Stott, theologian

Fortunately for man, in the divine economy, although man struck first to create conflict, God reaches out to resolve all three kinds of deathly separation so that man does not have to "do the time for his crime." A man may die physically but he does not have to die eternally.

Let us review the reasons why God must resolve man's conflict. These reasons find their source in the divine courtroom. The first reason concerns the nature of God. In His universe He demands that wrongs must eventually be righted because He will not circumvent or deny His justice. If God resolves man's transgression(s) without a worthy payment, He would be acting in an unjust way, something that He will not do.

The second reason concerns the nature of man. Man, the offender, cannot reconcile with God unless he satisfies

God, the offended one. The works of man lack the worth required for a payment to God to satisfy the judgment of the divine court. He must repay God but the payment that imperfect, rebellious, finite man would offer cannot suffice. Man has caused his problem and man lacks the standing and the ability to solve it.

God cannot wink at man's offense(s) and man cannot satisfy God's demands. The infinitely just God demands a payment, without blemish, 100 per cent pure, to meet His penalty. No man of earth can satisfy such a demand. The death that we die cannot satisfy him because it lacks worth. The human capital that he accepts must be pure and divine for the penalty that He levies. Only God Himself can overcome such bad news by resolving the conflict that sin has birthed.

Why must God put on flesh?

* *Only God can satisfy His own standard of justice.*

* *Only God would reach out in love to do that.*

His reaching out translates into a reaching down. He does this through the mystery of incarnation. To meet the divine standard for man, God must face death as a perfect man since only such death would satisfy His justice. He puts on flesh, dwells among man and dies as a substitute in man's place to provide a satisfaction or atonement for man. Through this act of reconciliation he will create a friendship with the sinner and eventually transform the one whom He redeems.

How can this be possible? How can God die?

Anselm, Archbishop of Canterbury in the 11th Century, put it this way when he wrote about the divine nature of the payment. Man's resolution of sin and death depends upon a satisfaction "which God only can, and man only should, make." He concluded that "it is needful that it should be made by one who is both God and man."

God also acts with consistency. On the one hand, as the divine Judge, He holds without wavering to a standard of unbending, exacting justice that cannot overlook man's debt because of sin. On the other hand, as the divine Lover, He will pay the debt by providing a payment to satisfy His own justice. It can be summarized in the following:

We offer imperfect performance; He offers perfect performance.

We cannot offer holiness; He offers holiness.

We offer unrighteousness; He offers righteousness.

Why is only God's work acceptable as the means to worth?

The infinite, just, holy God demands an infinitely holy sacrifice, without blemish to meet His demands. Only a perfect man could die; only God's blood satisfies God and has efficacy for all. The incarnation is a divine necessity if man can know God. To redeem man from his present and future dilemma, only God Himself can satisfy His own standard of divine justice and only God Himself could then loan to man His only worthy payment as He freely seeks to redeem.

If the preceding is true, no other way works. Unrighteous man dies because of his transgressions yet the righteous God is willing to die to pay for man's transgressions. He does that through a substitute. According to the previous thoughts, who would qualify as that substitute?

Who qualifies as the Savior?

A Christian world-view argues that only one person in history qualifies as that substitute: the Lord Jesus Christ. Jesus Christ is fully Deity; He is God. Jesus Christ is fully man; He is perfect man. He is the God-Man. He is eminently and solely qualified to be the Savior of the world. As God, Jesus Christ can satisfy the divine standard. As perfect man, Jesus Christ fulfilled the law completely. He was perfectly obedient to God. This proves His righteousness. It would be unjust to put him to death but he could die for sinners in their place.

The Son of God must put on the clothes of a human body because no other solution will work. During the Civil War, a wealthy citizen could avoid enlistment in the Union Army by paying another person to go in his place. That person who went would then act as the draftee's substitute. One such wealthy draftee told a poignant story of the substitute who died in battle for him. The draftee paid for the funeral and burial of the substitute. On the soldier's tombstone, he had these words chiseled: "He died for me." In his place, the man had died.

Christ acts as a substitute.

When God reaches out and down to man, He also gives worth to the offender's life by permitting the offender to cross over the gulf of estrangement that enmity has created and to know Him. Man also receives the added worth of a life-long transformation that God guarantees to His former enemies whom He now counts as His true friends.

> *"He [God the Father] has made Him [the Lord Jesus Christ] to be sin who knew no sin that in Him we might become the righteousness of God."* (2 Corinthians 5.21)

9

The Incarnation of the Son of God

- *A savior must be a perfect man to satisfy the standard as a man.*

- *A savior must be wholly God to satisfy the divine standard.*

How shall we now think about this proposal to escape death? As we have implied earlier, defining a problem well can lead to solving a problem well. A Christian world-view presents man as fabulous and fallen; as kind and cruel; and as one who blesses and one who curses. As a creation, man began as an untested and innocent creature who could bless God and who could bless fellow humans. After man fell, he began to exercise his capacity to be cruel and to curse God and others.

Man now finds himself in an abnormal position today. He retains God's image though marred that he originally received in the Garden; yet, he does not submit to or honor the One whose image he bears.

Other narratives make proposals to escape death and you may have considered one of these alternatives and even have adopted one. Many folks fail to consider any sort of proposal about death. You may have previously rejected this one because of misinformation or misunderstanding. No sane person would deny that death will get its due.

Without a true narrative that explains why our cherished life has a terminus and gives us hope beyond this physical death, how do we determine what has worth? How can this life be lived meaningfully?

Why should we examine and test this Christian world-view?

We live in many ironies in the world today. We may have the quickest means of communication but we do not have deep relationships of those who receive almost instantly our oftentimes inane messages. We remain well-connected but not well-related. Another irony has to do with work and free time. We have so many conveniences that permit us to have much more time than any previous generation. We possess this *extra* time and yet fail to set aside the time to consider what our brief time of living means.

At some point—and hopefully not on death's bed—we must think about a solution to death and find a solution that gives hope beyond our death bed.

Deep down inside we think that we do matter, that this life has a meaning to it beyond the grave and that this life ought not to end as it does. Unless we find and adopt a solution to resolve death and to explain the suffering because of it, we can neither find true purpose nor live in a way that has eternal worth.

Statements that we cannot completely prove take on the label of pre-suppositions. This does not necessarily mean that the statements lack validity. It also does not mean that these pre-suppositions lack some basis of proof. Without a direct plea to you, we have asked you to set aside your presuppositions that oppose this Christian world-view, temporarily suspend your disbelief about it and give it a thorough and thoughtful hearing.

This solution needs careful consideration since the idea presents Christian theology or what we may call historic Christianity. You may have disbelieved historic Christianity without having sufficient evidence to disbelieve. You may have disbelieved because of some Elmer Gantry type preacher who has offended your sense of reality. You may have disbelieved because of zealous Christians who lack compassion.

Or, more critically, you choose to disbelieve because your present lifestyle on this earth would be jeopardized if you consider and accept these pre-suppositions. [By the way, if you do think that way, then you have made progress about your understanding of a Christian world-view. A faith in Christ will bring change.] This world-view also needs careful consideration because it could mean the difference between a life of meaning and a life without meaning.

Eventually you will want to examine all the objections or doubts that you have about historic Christianity. These objections or doubts force us to fully assault our view and, if that view survives, to be more committed to it. Right now, however, the major focus comes down to a consideration of the one upon whom validity of historic Christianity rests.

Without the worth of His works,

you cannot possess eternal worth.
Without the worth of His works,
you cannot escape the judgment of God.

God's Son: His nature as a man

According to the New and Old Testaments of the Bible, only one person in all of history qualifies to save man from sin and the wages of death that it brings. The Lord Jesus Christ qualifies as that one. Let's consider Jesus the Messiah.

What evidence do we have that this Jesus of Nazareth actually existed? Let's look first at the so-called collateral evidence. What do contemporaries outside of the Christian faith or the Bible say about the existence of Jesus?

What do secular historians say?

Tacitus (AD 56—117), the Roman historian, reports in AD 64 that Nero "fastened the guilt" of the burning of Rome to the group who called themselves Christians and who believed in "a most mischievous superstition." Tacitus explains that this group's "Christus" [Latin for Christ] had suffered "the extreme penalty" by Pontius Pilate. The mischievous superstition as Nero sarcastically called it meant the belief that this Christ had risen from the grave.

The extreme penalty in the Roman law would refer to the hanging on a cross. Tacitus assumes that this "Christus" actually existed and received from Pilate, a real person in history, the penalty of crucifixion, an awful death at a certain place in real time in history past. Nero saw that these Christians would not recant and he even used some of them as torches to light his evening parties.

Pliny the Younger served as the Roman governor in Bithynia [present day Turkey] under Emperor Trajan. His province contained a large group of Christians, as he said, of every age and social standing who met together in their false religion. In AD 114 he wrote a letter to the emperor to find out how to proceed legally against the "Christians" [an illegal religion until AD 323]. According to the letter, these Christians "... were in the habit of meeting on a certain fixed day before it was light, when they sang in alternate verses a hymn to Christ, as to a god..."

In this example, Pliny notes that they did worship a historical person whom they called Christ. He also observed that the group considered this Christ to be a god. In response to these troublesome Christians, Trajan had this advice in his return letter, "whoever denies that he is a Christian and really proves it—that is, by worshiping our gods—even though he was under suspicion in the past, shall obtain pardon through repentance." Trajan and Pliny both assume that these "Christians" worshipped this Jesus as a god and not as the only true God.

Josephus [AD 37–100], the noted Jewish historian of the first century, makes an important observation about the historicity of Jesus. Twice in his accounts he mentions Jesus. In his *Antiquities*, Josephus speaks about James, "the brother of Jesus, the so-called Christ." The Great Sanhedrin, the so-called Supreme Court of ancient Israel, had condemned James to death. We learn from Josephus of the existence of both James and his brother Jesus who claimed to be the Christ [the anointed one or Messiah of Israel]. On another occasion, in *Testimonium Flavianum* [Testimony of Flavius Josephus], Josephus spoke of Jesus in this way, "About this time there lived Jesus, a wise man…" He also goes on to say that "Pilate had condemned him to be crucified."

This in no way suggests that Josephus considered Jesus to be God. Josephus just reports the facts. Because Josephus comes across as an objective viewer, his observations do argue for the existence of Jesus.

What does the Old Testament prophet Isaiah say?

One verse in the Old Testament of the Bible puts together the idea that the Savior of the world must be divine and must be human. The ancient scribes or keepers of the Hebrew text meticulously copied what the authors had written originally. They held the text in high regard and worked diligently not to make errors in their copies. This still holds true today for many Jews who have a high regard for their Scripture and its accompanying commentaries although they would interpret this verse differently than those who see Jesus as the fulfillment of this passage.

> "For unto us a child is born, unto us a Son is given;
> and the government shall be upon His shoulders;
> and His name shall be called
> Wonderful Counselor, The Mighty God,
> The Everlasting Father, and the Prince of peace."
> (Isaiah 9.6)

Commentators of different theological persuasions disagree about whom this verse refers. Conservative scholars who have adopted historic Christianity see this prophecy as being fulfilled in Jesus. Our point here has to do with how Isaiah argues for an incarnate God who can dwell among us in time, in a real place and in history to eventually fulfill all His roles.

What do the New Testament writers say?

Let's look at the New Testament documents as evidence of the existence of Jesus. These documents have as much reliability in terms of numbers of surviving copies of manuscripts and early dates as other ancient documents that we readily accept as historically reliable. In fact, in comparison to other ancient documents, we have much greater evidence because we have numerous copies of parts of the New Testament. Although Julius Caesar died in 44 BC, the earliest copies of his writings can be dated back only to AD 900. In contrast, parts of the earliest New Testament copies go back to the first century in which the original ones were written.

The physician Luke investigated the story of Jesus and spoke of his procedure when he wrote to a high ranking official by the name of Theophilus around AD 60. As he says,

> *"Forasmuch as many have taken in hand to set forth in order a declaration of those things which are most surely believed among us, Even as they delivered them*

unto us, which from the beginning were eyewitnesses, and ministers of the word; It seemed good to me also, having had perfect understanding of all things from the very first, to write unto you in order, most excellent Theophilus, that you might know the certainty of those things, wherein you have been instructed." (Luke 1.1-4)

Luke, as an ancient historian, adopted methods that true journalists and researchers practice today. They might also envy him. He adopted an orderly method of research. He spoke to eyewitnesses and he intended to be careful about what he reported. Even today no one has discovered an error in the history that he reports in terms of names and places. He wanted Theophilus to know the truth exactly about Jesus.

In his gospel volume, he begins his narrative even before the birth of Jesus as he gives background in detail. He then delivers what has become the well-read King James translation of the passage of the Christmas narrative when the angels address the shepherds.

"'For unto you is born this day in the city of David a Savior who is Christ [Messiah or anointed one] the Lord. And this shall be a sign unto you: You shall find the babe wrapped in swaddling clothes, lying in a manger." (Luke 2.11-12)

Later, in the narrative, Luke records how the obedient family took their newborn baby to the Temple to offer a sacrifice as required in Israel according to the Mosaic Law.

"At the end of eight days, when He was circumcised, He was named Jesus, the name given by the angel who had appeared to Mary, his mother before He was conceived in the womb." (Luke 2.21)

Both secular and sacred writings testify as witnesses to the existence of Jesus of Nazareth. They reveal that this Jesus did exist as a man who walked in a place on earth that many of us may have visited. In terms of history, the place of Israel where Jesus walked yet holds a regular and strong hold in daily newscasts.

God's Son: His nature as God

Secular writings may speak of Jesus as a man. Even Islam recognizes the existence of Jesus but only see him as a man, a prophet and a messenger of God. Islam would not see him as the Son of God and definitely not God incarnate. Our evidence for his deity rests solely but not unreliably on the ancient documents of the New Testament.

What does the apostle John in the New Testament say?

The apostle John, an original follower of Jesus, had this to say about Jesus:

"In the beginning was the Word, and the Word was with God, and the Word was God." (John 1.1)

"And the Word was made flesh, and dwelt among us, (and we beheld His glory, the glory as of the only begotten of the Father,) full of grace and truth." (John 1.14)

When you combine these two verses, you come to the conclusion that John recognized Jesus as both God and man. John also reports a quote where Jesus claims to be eternal in his existence.

"Jesus said unto them, 'Verily, verily, I say unto you, Before Abraham was, I am.'" (John 8.58)

John informs us in that same chapter about the angry and disputative response of the Pharisees, the conservative Jewish leaders of their day.

"Then they took up stones to cast at Him; but Jesus hid himself and went out of the Temple." (John 8.59)

They intended to execute Jesus and in violation of Roman law because they considered His speech as blasphemy in that He argued for an eternal existence when He said that He existed before Abraham. By using the phrase "I am," He identified himself with the phrase that God gave to Moses as the name of God when God spoke from the burning bush. They may have disliked and denied what Jesus said but they did understand his claim. They heard it rightly. They had no mistake about what He meant. He made the claim to be God.

What does the apostle Paul say?

The apostle Paul has left many epistles or letters to the early followers of Jesus. In this passage, the apostle refers to Jesus as deity when he uses the word "image" in the English or *eikon* in the language of the New Testament.

> *"And He [Jesus] is the image of the invisible God..."* (Colossians 1.15)

One of the earliest church statements of commitment about Jesus—the Apostles' Creed—said it this way:

> *"I believe in God, the Father Almighty, the Creator of heaven and earth, And in Jesus Christ, His only Son, our Lord; who was conceived of the Holy Spirit, born of the Virgin Mary, Suffered under Pontius Pilate, was crucified, died, and was buried."*

What did Jesus say about himself?

When Jesus spoke to a disciple just prior to His death, He said,

> *"'I am the way, the truth, and the life: no man comes to the Father, but by Me.'"* (John 14.6)

Before Jesus raised Lazarus, Jesus spoke with Martha, the sister of Lazarus,

"'I am the resurrection, and the life; he who believes in Me, though he dies yet shall he live. And whosoever lives and believes in Me shall never die. Do you believe this?' She said to him, 'Yes, Lord. I believe that you are the Christ, the Son of God who came into the world." (John 11.25-27)

How much do we need to know about Jesus?

This mystery of God's incarnation lies beyond the grasp of our understanding. The finite cannot fully comprehend the infinite; the fallen cannot truly understand the work of God. We all lack complete knowledge. When we board the plane or swallow our prescription drugs or even eat the preservative laden microwave food that we call fast food, do we think about consequences? Man can know some things well but he cannot know all things perfectly.

None of these mysteries sits atop the mystery heap like this mystery of incarnation. While the mystery of the incarnation may be beyond our understanding, the incarnation does not go against our understanding. In other words, we cannot explain how God can create and confine himself to holy and perfect flesh but we can make a reasoned and valid decision to accept the divine incarnation as a necessary and only solution to man's estrangement.

In brief, the only Son of God leaves heavenly dwellings and invades earthly history. Jesus Christ is fully Deity; He is God. Jesus Christ is fully man; He is perfect man. He is the God-Man. He is eminently and solely qualified to be that sacrifice and to save sinners by offering His life as a substitutionary sacrifice. Without this incarnation, no person can end estrangement from God, count God as his friend, and have an added worth now.

To understand historic Christianity we need to know at least this much:

* *Who Jesus is and*

* *What Jesus did.*

There's more to consider so that you may be sure about your rejection or acceptance of this world-view as a solution to death later and a way to live now.

10

Reprisal: How Do We Survive Eternal Death?

"There is no death of sin without the death of Christ."

JOHN OWEN, OXFORD PURITAN, 1616-1683

No one on earth knows all the people who acted as heroes to save those inside of the Twin Towers in New York on September 11, 2001. We have heard of the 411 professional rescuers such as firemen and policemen who had chosen such careers to protect and to serve others. Because of their choice and training they automatically rushed into the buildings and died in their attempt to save others. We now know that some in the Twin Towers escaped death that day because they embraced a ready savior. One executive testifies to her escape from the South Tower because of a man whom she identified only by the red bandanna that he wore on his face. Others speak about the mysterious man with the red bandanna who steered others to safety with multiple trips as he cried out, "This way to the stairs!" One woman followed him to safety as he carried another woman on his back.

Eventually the parents of this "volunteer" rescuer who worked on the 104th floor as an equity trader recognized him as their son, 24 year old Welles Crowther, a Boston College graduate. As an elementary school student their son began to carry a red bandanna daily. At age 16, he joined his father as a volunteer fireman in Nyack, New York. The last of the twelve (or eighteen) persons whom he rescued and saw him as he ascended back up for the final time into the smoking building said, "… he didn't save himself." The Fire Department of New York awarded him the first posthumous distinction as an honorary member of the New York Fire Department.

Those eighteen or so people escaped the tower that day because the man who led them to safety risked his life and eventually sacrificed his life to save that many in just 55 minutes, the length of time from the moment of attack to the moment of the tower's demise. Like most heroes he received his honor after he did his deed and left this earth.

We have muffled if not perverted the meaning of the word *hero* by carelessly applying it to public figures such as athletes or recovering addicts or even repentant celebrities. Strictly speaking a hero saves the life of another and may risk or lose his life in that act. Many times such heroes come as unlikely volunteers or so-called ordinary folks who excel beyond what others expect. The late Welles Crowther deserved every bit of the honorable title of hero.

We cannot know and we must not judge the motives or the commitment of this September 11 hero. Most likely, we could assume that those whom Crowther rescued he did not know nor with whom he had a relationship. He chose to rescue fellow living humans and neglected inanimate commercially valuable stuff. More importantly, he had no regard for his life.

In the strict sense of the word, Jesus came as a hero and we can judge His motives and His commitment. Jesus came to obey and to honor the Heavenly Father by doing His work on the cross for sinners' salvation. Jesus comes as a rescuing, resurrected hero to redeem those who will become His friends.

In the case of Jesus He knows us and does have a relationship to us but only as a Creator to creature and not as a Redeemer to the redeemed until He befriends us. With a motive to honor God the Father by His work on the cross as a sacrifice for sin and a commitment to sinners, Jesus, the divine-human Hero rescues sinners from the obstacles of estrangement from God—our twin towers of sin nature and sinful behavior.

We must embrace this salvation because our estrangement opposes the purpose of our creation since God designed us to be in a relationship with Him. This lack of connection with Him produces a lack of connection with others. From the seed of this estrangement a person reaps a harvest of all other kinds of problems internally with oneself and externally with others: lying, anger, denial, theft, murder, adultery, greed (just to mention a few).

We may be well-connected virtually by quickly communicating our trivial facts and casual thoughts through our hand-held devices of communication but we may lack the face to face ongoing encounters of communication that true friendship demands.

These behaviors confirm an honest person's unspoken suspicions—deadly actions reveal dark hearts. And a dark heart may be a dead heart. We may be alive physically but we are dead spiritually. His mercy convicts us of this our wretchedness—the standing and state of acting as and really being miscreants, breakers of God's law. This standing and behavior are the ultimate causes of our deaths.

Such bad news cannot deny the good news of historic Christianity. The infinite Creator has demonstrated that He is there for His creation and that He has spoken so that man, a finite creature made in His image, may hear.

Why is everyone not a friend of God?

The answer to this question comes straightforwardly: not every person accepts this solution. From eyewitness accounts, we know that many in the twin towers chose not to follow Crowther. Others hid out in the building and protected themselves. Others may have stayed because they understood that choice to be the best choice until firefighters came to rescue them. They could not or would not recognize Crowther as the one who knew the way to escape.

How does the sinner escape from estrangement that leads to destruction? Estrangement ends and friendship begins when the payment of God's sacrifice is applied in time. In the past at the cross the payment was made but it only gains effect in the present when a person believes. A person must repent or change his mind about his sin, quit trusting self and trust God. He must rely upon the sacrifice of the God-Man to satisfy or appease God. He must trust the Lord Jesus Christ as a substitutionary sacrifice to pay for his sins. Until that happens, a person remains spiritually dead, stands as God's enemy, is estranged from Him and will die eternally.

Chuck Colson, Watergate co-conspirator and chief trickster of the Nixon White House, once said, "I would run over my grandmother for Nixon." Later he admitted before the court his intentional unlawful conduct. In spite of that confession he did not think that he had sinned against God and was even estranged from Him. After he came out of prison for pleading guilty to a lesser crime, he went from infamous to famous as he created a global organization to rehabilitate ex-prisoners.

What made him realize his sin before God? That realization had nothing to do with drinking or smoking or immorality but pride. As a confidant of a successful, powerful politician, he lived a life full of pride. He recognized his true moral guilt before God for his position as a proud sinner and finally understood that only the work of Christ could pay for his sins. He then made a conscious and reasoned choice to rely upon Jesus Christ to pay the penalty that God demanded.

Intentionally and unintentionally we have sinned against the Almighty God. Like Colson, each of us has that one sin that sticks out that reminds us that underneath it all, we have true moral guilt before God.

No one but God Himself can provide the great escape from death. To escape eternal death and become a friend of the living God, God has to loan man the sacrificial payment of His Son. As the New Testament argues,

> *"He made Him who knew no sin to be sin on our behalf that we might become the righteousness of God in Him."* (2 Corinthians 5.21)

In reconciliation God declares the unrighteous His friend and enlivens that person because only spiritually alive people can know God. This act of enlivening or spiritual birth gives man the necessary ability and standing to commune with the living Lord and by His Spirit live out a life pleasing to Him and satisfying to us.

> "... *unless one is born from above, he cannot see the kingdom of God.*" (John 3:3)

Genuine faith in the promise of God's provision of a Savior provides the foundation for that enlivening. Faith in Him rests on the promise that God accepts the work of the Lord Jesus Christ as the only substitute in His death, burial and resurrection for our sins. Like those who found themselves trapped in that tower with no way out, a hero had to find them and direct them to the escape. Sinners must also be found and shown the escape from the entrapment of sin.

What can the Hero of the Christian world-view do?

That hero has come and He is the escape. The parents of the 911 hero found out later that in the last moments of their son's life he had given his life away so that others might go on living on earth. Jesus gave His life away so that we might live well now on this earth by His enablement and live with God forever because He has satisfied the divine penalty that would bring eternal death. His resurrection proves that the Son has satisfied God the Father.

If this pre-supposition or assertion of truth about life and God holds true, then God accepts only one kind of sacrifice. That one unique sacrifice upholds his justice and guarantees His righteousness. Only one unique person qualifies as that sacrifice—the Lord Jesus Christ. It would be unjust to put Christ to death if He is perfect. It is not unjust and indeed loving if He dies in our place as a satisfaction for our sins. Only the sacrifice of God could have efficacy for all.

A Christian world-view argues that the incarnation of God is a divine necessity. Only God meets God's standard and only a perfect man could die as a substitute for other men. God acts as subject; we assume the role of objects. Only Christ dies a death that satisfies God. We cannot die our death to satisfy Him because our death lacks worth.

He initiates; we respond. He offers His worth; each of us must make a choice about His worth that works to satisfy God. We can escape the bad news by embracing the good news. Most importantly, the great escape connects us to a great Friend.

11

How Will We Make A Decision?

"...I am incurably convinced that the object of opening the mind, as of opening the mouth, is to shut it again on something solid."
G. K. Chesterton, British writer

When the early church sent the apostle Paul to the ancient city of Berea in present day Greece, his companion Luke observed the noteworthy manner of the Bereans who challenged the truth of the statements of the apostle Paul:

> *"These [the Bereans] were more noble than those in Thessalonica, in that they received the word with all readiness of mind, and searched the scriptures [the Old Testament] daily to see whether these things were so."* (Acts 17.11)

On an earth of some 7 billion people, who can count the many paradigms of life or world-views that exist and have crept into every culture? We may not have adopted intentionally our world-view, but each of us lives according to some sort of overall framework. We present this world-view as the best and only narrative to understand worth, life, and death.

In spite of this truth claim, no one should move quickly from their view of life especially if they have thought long and hard about it. Most of us dislike arguments that threaten the beliefs that we hold dearly and may have inherited passively or determined casually. We naturally and rightly reject beliefs that oppose our own. What commitment to his own views does a person have if he quickly rejects his own personal belief system?

The process of the adoption of any idea ought to begin with the prospect that the idea ought to be rejected. Later, over a time of mental simmering and possibly emotional wrestling that person then re-considers this new and most likely disparate idea. On the other hand, a mature thinker ought not to be put off by a view that strongly opposes his view because it will push him to think in a way that would bolster or firm up his long-held paradigm of life and God.

In terms of our earlier discussion, a Christian worldview answers the tests for truth in this way:

1. In terms of *undeniability*, it presents a reliable and inspired record that reveals the incarnation, death and resurrection of a Savior, the God-Man, who came in a specific time, to a real place and left verifiable evidence.
2. In terms of *consistency*, it presents God as a transcendent Creator who can therefore give order and meaning to everything. It presents God as a personal Redeemer who can therefore relate to man.

3. In terms of *evil*, it presents God as one who shares a nature with us and qualifies to resolve the evil of death and its accompanying suffering.
4. In terms of *hope*, it guarantees a life beyond the grave by the power of a resurrected Savior and a life now of meaning to serve Him.

What makes a Christian world-view different?

Historic or traditional Christianity does not excuse man for his lawlessness neither does it deny man a solution to his lawlessness. We can look to the historical past to explain the present and to prepare for a future of hope. Man simultaneously stands as an image-bearer and as an image-breaker. Our design speaks of His wonder in making us; our deeds speak of our choices in marring us.

Buddha may define Buddhism. Mohammed may define Islam. Vishnu and other gods could define Hinduism. All religions have a founder somewhere upstream in its origin. Christianity certainly has a founder but its founder dies on a cross as an accused criminal. God the Father counts his death as a worthy payment for all who believe in His Son. His resurrection provides proof that we have hope beyond the grave.

God befriends the formerly spiritually dead offender-enemy who now lives forever as the friend of God. In spite of the greeting card industry and phone texting with the closing of "BFF," Best Friend Forever, human friendships may not be forever. Friendships end and friends do die. In terms of God, the initials have meaning and value. Friendship with God lasts forever and acts as the footings upon which the whole structure of other added worth is built.

Nothing on earth has more worth than to know God as your friend. Without intending to sound profane, He is the BFF for those who know Him.

Many would find this proposal about death and its cause as ridiculous or far-fetched or even fear-producing. You may not accept these ideas but, at the least, you will finally know what a Christian world-view really has to say about life and God.

A Christian world-view says that only Christ who is very man and very God can grant us an escape from death. If this world-view does not speak the truth, what view does? Without friendship with God through the death of Christ, how do you answer the following questions?

How else do you honor God as God?

How else do you solve the problem of evil in the world?

How else do you return man to the purpose of His design?

How else do you bring hope to the dying and add worth to the living?

It comes down to this when Pontius Pilate, the governor of Judea around AD 33, said to Jesus, "... *What is truth?*"

What did Pascal bet?

"It is not a tragedy to die for something you believe in, but it is a tragedy to find at the end of your life

that what you believed in betrayed you."

Joan of Arc

"I have been out in space and didn't see god; therefore, there is not a god."

Yuri Gagarin, Soviet cosmonaut and first man in space

Blaise Pascal, the French mathematician, philosopher and follower of Jesus, argued that, if the existence of God is a 50/50 chance, then it makes more sense to believe that He exists than not to believe that He exists.

Pascal states the wager of your life in this way. If God exists and you choose to believe in Him, then you may suffer now because of your obedience to Him but you will be able to enjoy God and His presence forever. On the other hand, if God does not exist and you believe in Him, you only miss out on meaningless pleasure but you will have lived an upright life which does benefit you and others.

Pascal's wager reminds us that we cannot be casual about this decision. The world-view that we adopt has present and, most importantly, eternal consequences. Our thoughts about life and God come as a weighty decision.

What did Jonathan Edwards argue?

Many historians have considered Jonathan Edwards (1703-1758) as one of the greatest intellects that America has produced. This Calvinistic preacher was eventually dismissed from his pulpit for his biblical view of salvation. He went to minister to the Housatonic tribes before he assumed the Presidency of Princeton University. He died because of a fever when he volunteered to test the new smallpox vaccine.

However, not that many years ago, high school students of literature would know him for his sermon on July 8, 1741 that he read from a manuscript in his pulpit to his church congregation during the Great Awakening, a time of epic public spiritual renewal in colonial America. The title suggests the heavy nature of his sermon: "Sinners in the Hands of an Angry God."

Unfortunately, like many explanations of the Christian world-view, literature books failed to tell the whole story since they included only part of the sermon. My literature had only the part about the judgment of God that Edwards displayed with very strong but clear illustrations.

Modern man fails to accept all the attributes of God. When it comes to God, they only want to hear about his love. Edwards may no longer be examined as an example of good American literature because textbook writers focused only on the judgment of God that Edwards stressed. But, when Edwards addressed a church audience that apparently claimed to be Christians, he spoke both about the judgment of God and about the grace of God. What you decide about the sacrifice of Christ determines which attribute that you enjoy.

Note what Edwards said in a very long sentence about the nature of America at that moment and about the nature of God that Scripture presents.

"And now you have an extraordinary opportunity, a day wherein Christ has flung the door of mercy wide open, and stands in the door calling with a loud voice to poor sinners; a day wherein many are flocking to him and pressing into the kingdom of God; many are daily coming from the East, West, North and South; many that were very lately in the same miserable condition that you are in, are now in an happy state, with their hearts filled and with love to him that has loved them and washed them from their sins in his own blood, and rejoicing in hope of the glory of God."

Jonathan Edwards

12

How Do We Gain The Hope Of Worth?

Can we deny the inevitable conclusion?
Our life on this earth will end.

We will continue to sit in the dry dock of life if we seek worth in the things of this earth or in the people on this earth. Trophies will tarnish; memories will fade; and strangers will eclipse our accomplishments. If we live long enough, we will lose our friends. Pursuits of things that fade or people that die cannot satisfy us yet we continue to pretend that they do.

Pursuits of possessions or achievements cannot add real worth to any one of us or ultimately put any one of us permanently above the rest of us. The illusion that promotion here on earth among the finite, by the finite and for the finite adds worth to life still remains an illusion and without genuine profit.

While God may seek, we hide in our earthly pursuits. In the book of Genesis in the Old Testament, God said to Adam in the Garden after he had sinned, "Where are you?" The context does not refer to the geography of the garden but the geography of his heart. Adam had left God behind.

How many of us have left God behind? Only one connection adds final and absolute worth to life. That connection must come from above—Creator to creature. Such worth finds its source in a friendship with God as Redeemer through the reconciliation that Christ brings.

No greater worth could one have than the possession of friendship with God. God's friend cannot add any more worth than God has already given. In fact, an attempt to add worth could meet the resistance of God. [But, that's another story.] God has reversed the process. Instead of a pursuit to add worth, God has pursued His friends and added His worth to them.

If you know God, what greater worth could you have than friendship with Him? What greater pursuit can there be than to know Him through His special revelation to us?

What will you do with the choice that concerns Jesus?

Many who say that they know God as their friend act as if they lack worth, walk without purpose and continue to pursue their course of adding worth to their lives through false and profitless pursuits. They continue to multiply trophies, seek experiences of pleasure and amass records of material. For you all who have developed this kind of spiritual amnesia, you must go back and *recognize* what kind of added worth God has added to those whom He calls His friends. You must return to the choice that you made to follow Jesus.

For you who have never considered the life of worth because you do not have God as your friend, consider this. If this Christian view of the world is true, you cannot escape the divine indictment of lacking His holiness but you can escape its divine execution. You may not avoid physical death but you can avoid eternal death. Faith in Jesus brings about the reconciliation by which He declares us righteous and we become His friend.

* *God solved the negative:*
  His just condemnation of us.

* *God delivered the positive:*
  our communion with Him.

The righteousness of God on loan from Him remains a mystery. God remains as God; man escapes his own evil and God now befriends him. When God reaches down to man that act describes grace. God puts on the clothes of perfect human flesh. We cannot fully understand this mystery of grace that the Son of God would humble Himself by confinement to a body of perfect flesh to redeem sinners from divine judgment but we can accept and trust with certainty this mystery of grace.

Summary of Part Two

Where's the worth?

In our private and honest moments, we could believe that our life will not end in nothingness and that we have meaning or purpose. In other moments, we may think as Peggy Lee mournfully and memorably sang,

> "Is that all there is?
>   Is that all there is?
> If that's all there is my friend
>   Then let's keep dancing
> Let's break out the booze
>   And have a ball
> If that's all there is."

A satisfactory understanding about life and worth cannot be found within ourselves. Unfortunately, as we sprint through full schedules, we have little time to think much about ourselves or our eternal future. As frustration through a variety of avenues arrives, we chase for and choose answers on the horizontal and transitory plane: new things, new friends, new spouses, new jobs, new drugs and new places. However, the answer lies beyond us. This proposed answer may sound religious but that answer does not lie in an institution or an organization but rather in a relationship—a relationship whose invitation we must not refuse lest we ruin ourselves forever.

Friendship with God grants true worth and an eventual added worth. Only this specific and certain kind of friendship—a friendship with God—adds worth to life and worth like no other. In our nation's capital success may depend not just upon your good ideas but upon whom you know. In terms of a Christian world-view, success in life depends upon an acceptance of the truth and faith in His Son that leads to a relationship with the Author of truth who has delivered His special revelation to us.

In short, an identity in Him gives a proper view of self because:

1. A finite creature needs an infinite point of reference that lies outside of the creature. We who are subjective need the One who is objective and can integrate and give meaning to all parts of life.
2. A fallen creature needs a divine person to meet God's standard for us and a perfect man to stand in our place before God.

3. Jesus Christ is not only that person as the God-Man but the point of reference around which to integrate and to give meaning to our lives.
4. When you place your trust in Jesus Christ, He then becomes your substitute to satisfy God's penalty, to grant you eternal life and to enable you to live out this life.

What choice do you have?

When it comes to choices, everyone wants options. Clear-cut decisions eventually come down to two quite disparate options. We call those kinds of choices a binary decision where the two options sit at opposite and opposing poles. In other words, either you choose Option A or Option non-A. No other choices can be made. Sometimes people make false binary decisions. This happens when Option B or option C may also be available and they do not know it. In the case of a Christian world-view, it comes down to a true binary decision.

Scripture makes it clear, Jesus said, "I am the way, the truth and the life…" The other pole or choice comes as "Jesus is not the way, not the truth and not the life…" Either we trust Jesus Christ or we do not trust Jesus Christ. From the perspective of a Christian world-view, no middle option comes into play.

We all tend to operate by "What's in it for me?" Well, what's in it for you? The "what" means a true and lasting worth. The true worth that works comes when God pays your debt by the worth of the atoning work of the Lord

Jesus Christ. A man can know God because he believes that Christ died as a substitute for his sins.

An understanding or enjoyment of life is found on the vertical and eternal plane. The meaning and enjoyment of life comes from a relationship with God who is there and who has spoken clearly in His Word about the revelation of His Son. Only the worth of Jesus Christ works to satisfy the Heavenly Father. Knowing Him has more worth than anything else. Only His worth works.

Can you find another way?
What keeps you from trusting Jesus?
How long can you wait?

"Believe in the Lord Jesus Christ and you will be saved…" (Acts 16.30)

Part Three: Worth Continuing

"Let me be taught that the first great business on earth is the sanctification of my own soul."

Henry Martyn, 19th Century missionary and linguist

"When Jesus Christ Himself ceases to be central in the life and loyalty of the Christian, the Christian becomes spiritually eccentric. Since his life is off center and out of focus, spiritual aberrations are inevitable."

Richard Halverson, 20th Century Presbyterian pastor and former chaplain of the U.S. Senate

One word distinguishes Christianity and pointedly sets it apart from all other religions or belief systems: relationship. Quite often those of the faith and even those outside of the faith present Christianity as solely an issue of eternal life. "If you trust Jesus, you will live forever and go to Heaven. If you do not trust Jesus, you don't go to Heaven."

While those statements have validity, this privilege to know the living Lord in a personal way cannot be set aside or neglected. While God has delivered the knowledge of Himself and His desires through His Word, God cannot be described as a set of principles or ideals. God has personhood. He desires to be known and we ought to seek Him as a Person.

Saints may falter and fail but this Savior will not. Our Redeemer intends to be serious about his relationship to those whom He has redeemed. A Christian world-view argues that God has offered Himself as He seeks out sinners. Knowing Him ranks as the first, best and overall worth that we can have on a daily basis now and not just later when we die.

In other words, God will love His redeemed ones as much on the day that they come to Him in ruin as He does on the day that they appear before Him in glory.

Most importantly, unlike other belief systems, the saint may draw near to God. He can draw near because the work of satisfying God had nothing to do with him but had everything to do with the work of Jesus upon the cross. He can draw near without fear because his brother Jesus has gone ahead as a great high priest to intercede for him. The mysterious, transcendent God permits access because

He has dwelt among us, left because of a finished work of divine worth and will return to establish forever with His brethren a perfect rule upon earth.

Both Martyn and Halverson speak strongly and clearly about the "business" [Martyn] of the Christian in sanctification and about the failing spirituality without Christ at the "center" [Halverson] of life. In spite of a grace generated eternal relationship with God, the saint has a responsibility to match deeds in this life with the decision that brought eternal life.

Those who have experienced God's work for them must begin to respond to God's work in them. Our external actions must match our internal faith. We must begin to work out in our experience that decision to which we made a commitment so that our behavior reflects our belief. Choices made privately to change where no one sees have to work their way out into the public where everyone sees.

Saints must move forward in faith because they cannot go back to their former selves. Just as we would not come to God without a revelation of Himself to us, neither can we grow without an appropriation of the scriptural revelation that He has delivered by His Spirit through His prophets and apostles. We cannot work out into our lives what we do not know. Until we know His Word and learn who God is and what He does, how can we act like Him? We give the name of "discipleship" to that process of moving forward to grow in faith.

Discipleship grounds saints in the faith. Discipleship closes the gap between belief and behavior. God calls the saint to work at the task of closing this gap between belief and behavior until the moment that he sees Jesus.

External performance founded on internal saving belief and by Spirit-enabled conviction proves to you your eternal profession. Added worth motivates the one who knows and follows Jesus to be responsible in making his believing faith also a behaving faith. Such added worth fundamentally comes through a study of and equipping from His Word.

How else can we know Him and know Him better except through His communication in His Word to us?

What will we do with the bestowal of worth?

"Just as I am, without one plea But that Thy blood was shed for me, And that Thou bidd'st me come to Thee, O Lamb of God, I come! I come!"

Charlotte Elliot, 19th Century hymn writer

Can you accept God's work of justification and not do your work of sanctification? We come to the Lord Jesus Christ just as we are no matter the extent of our sins. We come as unredeemed sinners. On the other side, as His friends, we cannot say any longer, "Just as I am." It must now be "just as He desires." We now begin an unending pursuit of finding out who He is and getting to know Him.

We must be diligent to discover what we ought to believe because we cannot behave in a Christian way until we believe Christian things. How can we know how to behave unless we know what we believe? The external Word objectifies what we believe; our external actions reveal our internal beliefs. Godly character brings forth godly behavior. Godly behavior must be built on obedience to His Word. Moreover, how can we have a growing relationship to God unless we know more about Him and about what He has done and what He is doing?

Nonetheless, in spite of the need to pursue knowledge of Him, we must not forget our identity and our worth. Who are we? We stand as saints who, by the grace of God, have met, know and have a relationship with the living Lord of the universe who created us and everything in the universe. That statement—no matter how much more we may know—we cannot forget. We cannot escape that standing in Him and must constantly reckon it as true in order to continue to work out in our daily living our salvation.

What worth do we have? In everyday earthly affairs, the wise person leaves a will or testament to declare who ought to receive his worth. A death must take place before the terms of that testament can be executed. Then the recipients know their inheritance. The same holds true in the arena of faith. His death executed His will or New Covenant. It certainly brought us the worth of a relationship to God but its other provisions bring us much added worth.

This worth that works ought to motivate us to live for Christ and to live out that life in Christ. The following chapters briefly explain some of the multiplied worth that God has granted to those who have by the gift of God placed their faith in His Son and now live as His heirs. What works will our borrowed worth produce? *Who are we and what do we have*?

13

The Added Worth of Justification

"For what does Scripture say, 'And Abraham believed God and it was reckoned to him as righteousness'."

Romans 4.3

"But to the one who does not work, but believes in Him who justifies the ungodly, his faith is reckoned to him as righteousness."

Romans 4.5

Justification by God adds worth to your life. The death of Christ settled once and for all the cosmic conflict that we began with God. That ended when He reconciled us. We owe that privilege to His justification of us. Justification means that, on the basis of the work of the Son in His death on the cross and our faith in the Son, He declares us righteous in Him. Out of that justification our sanctification or spiritual growth emerges. Without justification no saint would possess any eternal worth let alone added worth.

The concept of justification is not confined to theology and not unfamiliar to us. For instance, in printing, the left margin of the paragraph has a very straight line. Sometimes the right has a ragged and uneven edge. In that case, only the left is justified because all the sentences have been lined up with a *straight* edge. If you decide upon a course of action for business and you want a loan from a bank, then you must justify your reasons. You must prove that you have drawn the *right* conclusions. If the conclusions prove valid, then you may receive the loan because your reasons justify your cause.

Justification finds its origin and most familiar role in the judicial setting. So many necessary human transactions find their legitimacy on the basis of law. Legal controversy between parties requires judgment to set things right or to set things straight. Just societies establish courts where judges and/or juries rule on the rightness of a case.

Justification and judgment go together. They cannot be separated from each other. In civil cases, the party that wins his case may be said to have been justified in his cause. When the authorities charge a person with a crime, the jury must eventually deliberate and judge whether that person receives a justified verdict of "guilty" or "not guilty." The court will not render a pronouncement of "innocent" since the accused may have actually committed the crime but the evidence and/or the prosecutor fail to convince the jury.

This legal setting serves us well in understanding the theological view of justification. In the divine docket, man has no defense against his indictment of unrighteousness. Two different but related pieces of evidence convict us: judicial evidence and experiential evidence. Biblical Christianity speaks of a literal Adam who disobeyed God in the Garden of Eden and suffered the judgment of God because of that decision. The consequences of that decision have affected us all. As unfair as it may seem, Adam represented all mankind. When God imputed or reckoned Adam's sin to his account he also reckoned it to the account of every human.

The second piece of evidence comes from our own experience. From Adam our original earthly "father," we have also inherited an imperfect or sinful nature. The possession of such a nature does not prevent us from doing good things. Man may live in a fallen state but he does have freedom to create fabulous things and to achieve incredible goals like landing on the moon or inventing a computer.

But such a nature does prevent a person from possessing the desire or ability to live as God would demand. We act toward God and toward others in hurtful, self-serving and unloving ways. We act as lawbreakers in terms of His moral law. Both pieces of evidence confirm the verdict of guilty against each one of us. In both accounts—imputed sin in the divine accounting and inherited sin in daily living—we demonstrate unrighteousness.

As we have said before, no matter how hard we try we cannot attain by status or achieve by deed the righteousness that he demands. As short-comers in a fallen state of sinfulness, we cannot meet His holy law of perfection. No one can know God, go to Heaven or live a God-honoring life as long as he offends God. In God's court, the sinner can only enter a plea of "guilty."

Because of Adam's sin and our sins, we are not innocent. When God's gavel falls, He confirms our plea by declaring our verdict as guilty. In our standing and state of unrighteousness, we cannot receive anything but a guilty verdict in His holy court. That verdict also means that we deserve and will receive a capital punishment of eternal death or separation from Him. However, we can appeal His verdict but only in Christ as our advocate!

Too many of us fail to appeal to God or to think about our unrighteousness until we have to face tragic failures. When people speak of a near-death experience, they speak of how their life flashed before them. If they had time, they may also remember their unrighteous deeds that flash before them. They could even regret their shortcomings and pledge loyalty to God if He would just let them survive. We call such incident a "foxhole" conversion if later those same repentant folks try to act righteously but fail in that endeavor as they go back to their old unrighteous ways.

That does make perfect sense from a Biblical standpoint because no matter how hard we try, we lack the ability to be righteous. Until God declares you righteous, you cannot act righteously. We all face and practice a foxhole conversion unless we appeal to God according to His desires and in line with His just character.

In short, God cannot accept for the payment of sin any person's works because every person lacks the holiness that brings about works of perfection. Our unrighteous character cannot possibly produce righteous works that would satisfy His just standard.

On the other hand, we can appeal to God through the only way that He provides to satisfy His justice: the work of His Son—the God-Man—upon the cross. The reason that the friend of God has the added worth of justification has everything to do with Another's personal work and not his own personal works. As perfect man, Christ fulfilled the law completely. He was perfectly obedient to the law of

God. This proves His righteousness. It would be unjust to put him to death if he is perfect. As God, He satisfies the divine standard for as many as believe.

His death can satisfy justice for us if he died in our place. He is punished for us. When a person trusts or believes in Jesus Christ, the perfect and righteous work of Jesus Christ is imputed or put to his otherwise debt-ridden and unrighteous account. God's just standard is met for that person because Christ has become his substitute. Only by this divine accounting transaction of receiving the righteousness of Christ does the sinner gain a righteous standing before God.

During the American civil war, a wealthy person could escape President Lincoln's draft. He would do this by paying another to stand in his place in the draft and then serve for him. In one particular case, this substitute soldier died and the war had not yet concluded. The federal government then drafted the wealthy man and insisted that he serve. The man appealed in the federal courts and argued that he had already served through his substitute. Eventually, the courts agreed with the man. Because the substitute had served in his place, that substitute service satisfied the government's requirement.

Children love to dress up and pretend that they are what they wear. At the annual autumnal neighborhood costume parade, all kinds of pirates, cartoon characters, fairy tale folks and others appear and want others to regard them according to the clothes that they wear. Adults may dress up for costume parties just to escape temporarily from life and assume another persona for a moment.

In the case of those who trust in the righteousness of Christ, the clothes of righteousness that they wear they wear forever. The Son has secured His righteousness to loan to them—a loan we cannot and do not have to pay back. They do not have to pretend about their righteousness. God by His Spirit will enable His justified friends to match the inside of their lives with the outside clothes of righteousness that they wear.

Justification comes by the gift of faith as God Himself invades our personal space. No one finds justification—a declaration of righteousness—without God's gift of faith. [Romans 5.1; Ephesians 2.8, 9] No one has this gift until he makes a genuine choice to receive it. Without this justification, no other spiritual worth can God add to a person's life. Through this justification, the saint received reconciliation.

How ought we to view this justification?

* *He died while we were yet ungodly.*
  Romans 5.6

* *He died while we were helpless.*
  Romans 5.6

* *He died while we were sinners.*
  Romans 5.8

* *He died while we were his enemies.*
  Romans 5.10

* *He reconciled with his enemies. Romans 5.10*

Faith in the Lord Jesus Christ and his work of righteousness brings personal justification. In this transaction of justification God declares an unrighteous person as righteous. In the court of the Almighty Judge, a person receives an everlasting verdict of "not guilty". On the basis of Christ's work, God has acquitted the sinner and treats him as if he always possessed innocence. Through the instrument of faith, God puts to the debtor's account of unrighteousness His divine righteousness which is only and totally acceptable. God trades our sinfulness for His righteousness. God then always accepts these justified ones.

Others may accept His children conditionally or even reject them but the changeless One tenaciously grips those whom He has received. Long after the words and breath of this life fades, God's verdict of "not guilty" echoes eternally. Future trespasses can receive forgiveness through confession. Present and wrongful feelings of guilt can be discarded.

This justified person now legally and eternally enters the family of God as His child and as His friend. Because the infinitely worthy One, the Lord Jesus Christ, has placed His infinitely worthy work to the short-comer's account by faith, the short-comer has worth. The short-comer turned saint has worth not because of who he is but because of who Christ is. The short-comer now over-comer wears Another's clothes. Only these clothes permit admission to God's party. Without these clothes, no person gains admission to God's glory party of eternity—the enthronement of the Son.

Gaining the worth of justification by God comes as part of trusting Jesus Christ, His Son, who freely gave His life for us. Once the living Lord of the universe has declared us righteous, then we no longer need to pursue earthly worth. He has so multiplied our worth with acceptance by Him in the Son that we cannot add to that worth. Most importantly, we also cannot subtract from that worth. If a person has genuinely trusted Christ, then he possesses the righteousness of Christ forever. We can stand confidently before God the Father as if Christ's righteousness is our righteousness.

Unfortunately, you may not act justified. You then need to examine the added worth of the process of growth or sanctification. God has provided a righteous status. The Heavenly Father now sees the sinner not in his unrighteousness but in the righteous clothes of the Son. Now we respond to His work in us to strive for a righteous state in our daily living. In short,

Justification	**Sanctification**
brings membership into the family of God	cultivates communion with God
means an expression of faith that brings *a righteous standing*	means an expression of faith that brings *a righteous experience*
establishes the *root* of our spirituality	brings about the *fruit* of our spirituality
means the grace in which *we stand*	means the grace in which *we walk*

14

The Added Worth of Freedom

"Liberty consists in doing what one desires."
John Stuart Mill, British philosopher

"Stand fast therefore in the liberty where Christ has set us free, and be not entangled again with the yoke of bondage."
(Galatians 5.1)

When the astronauts landed upon the moon, they could jump higher and hit a golf ball farther than on earth. The moon provided a freedom of movement that the earth had denied. However, they lacked the freedom to move without living inside of a protective suit. Without that cumbersome cage to protect them from the outside elements and to provide the inside elements of life's oxygen, they would have no freedom of movement upon the moon. Death would deprive them of the freedom to live if they discarded that suit.

Only the imaginary comic book hero Superman could live in such outer space without the engineered inner space that the earth suit provides. As someone has pointed out, you can jump off a building and be perfectly free from gravity until you hit the ground. A finite creature lacks absolute freedom in the physical realm.

How does this culture view freedom?

Maybe, just maybe, freedom could come in the area of the metaphysical—the arena of thoughts and ideas. Those who want freedom from Biblical truth take the moniker of "free" thinkers. They would characterize Christians as those who have closed minds. Such free thinkers tend to be atheists, agnostics, cynics, pragmatists and rationalists. They may see no evidence for a resurrection let alone a savior. We presently live in a culture that promotes this kind of free thinking.

The 19th Century English philosopher Clifford said it this way, "It is wrong always everywhere, and for anyone, to believe anything upon insufficient evidence." Free thinkers come out of all kinds of venues: Charles Darwin, the proponent of natural selection; Nathaniel Hawthorne, the American author of *The Scarlet Letter;* John Adams, the second President of the United States; the much quoted poet, essayist and pantheist Ralph Waldo Emerson and Clarence Darrow, the famous American criminal lawyer who said, "I don't believe in God because I don't believe in Mother Goose."

Before we examine the added worth of freedom for the follower of Jesus, what kind of freedom do free thinkers want?

Janis Joplin, that soulful and sometimes screaming singer of acid rock, probably delivered the best interpretation of her friend Kris Kristofferson's song "Me and Bobbie McGee" whose refrain speaks of freedom as just a word for "nothing left to lose." As the lyrics say, "nothing may be worth nothing" but, at least "it's free." Sadly, in pushing the boundaries of the freedom of pleasure, Janis Joplin departed early and left nothing for her friends at age 27 when she died of a drug overdose.

Mario Savio, along with other so-called dissidents, in 1964, at the University of California at Berkeley, birthed the "free speech movement." He and others protested the whole educational philosophy that had characterized the university from its origin. One student held a sign that suggested the university respected data processing cards more than they respected students. "I am a UC student. Do not bend, fold, spindle or mutilate." These strikers held the idea that students ought to be consulted for curriculum choices and that the students could freely speak their views. All this took place ironically where students practically went to school for free.

The Free Speech Movement contributed to and mirrored the eventual state of cultural affairs in America today such as freedom from morality, freedom from law, freedom from responsibility, freedom from work, freedom from self-control. Those who engaged themselves in such protests used to say. "Never trust anyone over the age of thirty." Now that many of those have ages of twice that amount, they have found places in government, business, universities and churches where they continue to practice their kind of freedom and slowly infest the culture with this kind of freedom that God never intended.

For most of these free thinkers, freedom means the complete emancipation from any authority. For most of us, freedom means the separation from the distasteful, the uninviting, and basically anything that you do not want to do. Freedom, in the most basic sense of the word, means doing what I always wanted to do and no one can tell me not to do it.

The late federal judge and law professor Robert Bork describes the pursuit of personal freedom or liberty as never really having a terminus and "hostile to constraints." Bork said, "Men seek the removal of the constraint nearest them. But when that one falls, men are brought against the next constraint, which is now felt to be equally irksome." No one can satisfy himself with just a little bit of freedom.

In the final analysis we cannot be as free as we want because we would have to be in absolute control. We have enough trouble just having the freedom that we want even for a moment. Only a god could have such control. To attempt such control leads eventually to frustration and even to despair. At that point of admission that we lack control to gain freedom, we resign ourselves to ask, "What freedom do we have?"

How does freedom look for the follower of Jesus?

While these expressions of freedom may affect and even be practiced by Christians, these kinds of freedom have little to do with Biblical freedom. Freedom for the saint—

anyone who truly knows God through Jesus—has to do with liberation "from" and a submission "to."

Freedom means liberation "from" sin in the sense of performance. When the apostle Paul wrote to the church at Galatia, he briefly reviewed the spiritual history of the Galatian saints and, in turn, to any of us who have entrusted ourselves to Jesus Christ. Prior to faith, each of us lived outside but not beyond the saving grace of God. We acted as we were: lawless enemies of God. When grace came as He opened our hearts by the hearing of the gospel, God made us His friends and put us into His family.

The most fundamental problem for the saint then arose: forgetting how we got to be His friends. We and the Galatians got here by the worth of His Son's work. The Galatians drifted into this spiritual amnesia. They began to act as if they could impress God with their performance, especially in terms of what the Law had to say. They quit trusting Him for their worth and began trusting themselves for their worth. Using some biblical imagery in the letter, the apostle reminds the Galatians in a satiric way about how foolish they have been acting:

> *"I would like to learn just one thing from you, 'Did you receive the Spirit by works of the Law or by believing what you heard?'"* (Galatians 3.2)

The Law reminded us of our sin and the worthlessness of our works or performance to earn His gift of salvation. Our works even as a Christian cannot earn favor with God. If a saint comes to a saving knowledge by the Spirit through the gift of faith and not by his own works, how can the saint continue to act as if his works give him a better standing with God?

> *"Are you so unintelligent that you began by the Spirit and now you will finish by the flesh?"* (Galatians 3.3)

A freedom *from* sin in terms of justification also means a freedom *from* sin in terms of sanctification.

The saint comes to his freedom from the penalty of sin by faith; he must now live free from the power of sin by faith. In either coming to Christ initially or in living for Christ daily, the saint must cry out in weakness for the Spirit to enable him to manifest by faith a life in the Spirit.

Secondly, freedom for the saint means more than liberation *from* sin but also a submission *to* God. As ironic as it may sound, freedom for the Christian has its boundaries. A river runs best in its banks. A river's freedom does not apply to the river's flood. At that point, the river has reached beyond the freedom of its banks and destroys where it goes. This imperfect analogy does give some light to the role of God's friends in the world. The lives of the saints must flow within the boundaries that God has established for the current of their lives.

During the American civil war, both those in the North and in the South claimed that God was on their side. Someone asked President Abraham Lincoln which side God had joined. Lincoln apparently said, "Sir, my concern is not whether God is on our side; my greatest concern is to be on God's side, for God is always right." A person of character wants to be on God's side no matter the cost. That first came for the saint at the moment of faith when the sinner turned from self for salvation and turned to Him. After that singular point in time, the saint must resist drifting from God's will and sliding unto his own will.

True freedom relieves us from performance as an enslaving way to earn favor with God or to earn favor with others. It does not relieve us of our responsibility to serve Him. When it comes to freedom, He has not set us free to serve ourselves. He has set us free to serve Him. That service comes in the ambition that He has granted to be available to Him in a variety of venues.

Genuine freedom comes in living within the bounds that the Designer has drawn morally, physically, mentally and spiritually. No saint has the freedom to lie, cheat, steal, fornicate, drink excessively, or even rage against others. However, you do have the freedom to manifest His fruit or our virtue: love, joy, peace, patience, kindness, goodness, faithfulness, humility and self-control.

Gaining the added worth of freedom to serve God comes as part of trusting Jesus Christ, His Son. Only the one who knows the living and true God has true freedom—real freedom to escape these false concepts and to serve the genuine master.

A saint finds freedom in the following areas and more.

1. Freedom not to sin.
2. Freedom from condemnation.
3. Freedom to serve.
4. Freedom from performance.
5. Freedom to fail.
6. Freedom from control of outcomes.
7. Freedom from fear.

The friend of God finds himself with apparently conflicting identities. On the one hand, God has declared that His redeemed ones have the freedom of an heir. Through Christ Jesus we have access to the Father.

> *"And because you are sons, God has sent forth the Spirit of his Son into your hearts, crying, Abba, Father. Therefore you are no more a servant, but a son; and if a son, then an heir of God through Christ."* (Galatians 4.6-7)

On the other hand, a saint now has the status of a royal slave. A slave has the freedom only as the master gives. Those who translate the Greek New Testament into English have usually translated the word *doulos* [slave] as "servant" in most contexts. This translation diminishes the true import of this word. When you place your faith in Christ, you have not added some new or frivolous ideas to your life.

Instead, you have come to a brand new status and a radically different view of everything and everyone. Your thinking has to change. We must now define ourselves as being "in Christ." Being in Christ ought to mark all that we do in this life. The theologian Charles Ryrie summarized life in Christ in this way, "Salvation affects the whole man."

That great Interrupter, the Holy Spirit, brought you the gift of salvation in your justification. Now, that same Holy Spirit brings you the gift of ability in your sanctification. Just as a sinner implores God to save him, so also must the redeemed sinner ask God to enable him by His Spirit to serve. And he must make a choice as the song says to "trust and to obey." God-enabled behavior is accompanied by the genuine choices that we make.

This dual status of heir and of slave cannot be denied. A heir looks forward to the joy of a reward that rightfully belongs to him. A royal slave wants to live to please his master without regard to the reward but rather to the glory of his master.

15

The Added Worth of Ambition

"There is nothing more exciting in the world than to create something, to dig a foundation, to build a building on it."
C. Kemmons Wilson, founder of Holiday Inns

"Many people spend their lifetime indefinitely living."
Paul Tournier, Swiss physician and writer

Ambition fuels the drive to succeed. Throughout history, those who have succeeded in their respective fields of endeavor had to possess ambition. Even the most indolent among us has the potential of ambition. Ambition brings future, unseen vision into the present and then seen substance. Ambition pulls our vehicle of creativity forward to close the gap between dreams and reality. Ambition comes as part of the image of God though marred by sin that all humans possess. The One who created out of nothing has given us the permission to create out of His something.

The world has its fill of ambition. It led Alexander to conquer as much of the known world as he could before he died at the age of 33. It has characterized the founding of this nation. Not all settlers arrived as the Pilgrims did to worship in freedom but ambition has pushed the successes both negative and positive in our national establishment. Ambition has also brought about some of the worst evils in all the history of the world as conquerors and dictators have murdered even their own people for their own personal ambition.

Shakespeare put the words in his mouth but they certainly fit the climax of clashing ambitions as the slashing continued in the Forum. "Et tu, Brute," speaks Julius Caesar at his death as he discovers Brutus in a murderous coup. Ambitious men conspired in the assassination and his loyal supporter executed the coup. The idea of a "Brutus ambition" may seem far from us because we would not murder another; but, we must all guard against a Brutus type of ambition that eventually harms others in our path.

What characterizes legitimate ambition?

The English word *ambition* appears three times in the New Testament where it translates a Greek word that literally means "love of honor." In Romans 15.20, the apostle qualifies his ambition in terms of the gospel. He intended to go and preach the gospel where it had not yet been preached, "… to proclaim the gospel not where Christ is already proclaimed." He goes on to say that he would avoid such territory so that he would not be building on a foundation that someone else had already laid. This could imply that he had pride and intended not to cooperate with others; but, much more likely, he wanted to hurry to get the gospel out to the whole world and bypassed places where others had already established a gospel ministry. In this case, the apostle speaks of ambition in the sense of expanding the gospel.

In 1 Thessalonians 4.11, *ambition* is seen in regard to relationships. The context concerns life with those who know God and life with those who do not know God. Saints throughout Macedonia had heard of the continued sanctification of the Thessalonians. That sanctification had to do with their love of one another and with the faith that they demonstrated toward outsiders. In terms of the brethren, the apostle reminds those in Thessalonica to keep on loving one another. They required no exhortation to love one another since they practiced love toward one another already. The saints in Thessalonica understood that God has called His own to have relationships to others and to make it a paramount issue in the life of the saint.

In regard to the world outside of the church, the apostle reminded them to "make it your ambition to live quietly and work with your own hands." (1 Thessalonians 4.11) This reflects the apostle's earlier explanation of communicating the gospel. He said in the first chapter of the letter to the Thessalonians that he shared his life and his gospel with them. In other words, the apostle did not neglect relationships as he delivered the revelation of the gospel. He goes on to say about them "that you might walk honestly before outsiders and not be in need." (1 Thessalonians 4.11)

Others should not think that the gospel which they hear comes with a plea to pay. Too often the moniker of Christian is used by those who claim to know Christ to sell a product to others. Many businesses will put a cross or an equivalent symbol to let others know that they have a "Christian" business.

When it comes to the ambition of representing Christ to others outside of the body, character cannot be denied. Who can hear the words of our message if the ethics of our lives do not match the words of our speech? A flawed character could prove to be a stumbling block for the gospel. People ought to want to hear our message not because we say that we are Christians but rather because we act as Christians. Because He has loved us we must love others. This in no way implies that they will love us in return. Why should we expect more than Jesus received from the world? On the other hand, if a person comes to Christ, why would he not love the one who shared the blessed good news with him?

The third use of the word captures the nature of the life in Christ, "… we make it our ambition, whether in this body or away, to be pleasing to Him." (2 Corinthians 5.9) This phrase acts as a catch-all to encompass all that we do. We live and work for His glory. "Whether therefore you eat or drink or whatever you do, do all for the glory of the Lord." (1 Corinthians 10.31)

When it comes to a definition of glory, it challenges our thinking and we must look to examples for its understanding. When the angels announced the birth of Jesus to the shepherds, they said, "Glory to God in the highest and on earth peace with men whom He is pleased." (Luke 2.14) In the angels' context, "respect" or "honor" would define glory. The angels recognized that the arrival of the Son by His obedience to the Father would bring glory to God.

When God dwelt with Israel, He manifested His presence by His glory in the tabernacle in the wilderness and in the temple. When Jesus dwelt among the disciples, John wrote that "we beheld His glory, glory as the only begotten of the Father, full of grace and truth." (John 1.14) John saw the incarnate Son as manifesting the glory of God by His visible, fleshly presence among them. Pleasing Him means having motives and actions that give respect to Him.

Where does your ambition lead you?

Where would we be as a culture without people of ambition who persevere in a variety of professions? Since ambition usually brings success, we must be careful how we view ambition because success has its problems. C.S. Lewis reminded us that "prosperity knits a man to the world. He feels that he is 'finding his place in it,' while really it is finding its place in him."

Note how the apostle John warned us:

> *"Love not the world, neither the things in the world. If any man loves the world, the Father is not in him for all that is in the world—the lust of the flesh, the lust of the eyes and the boastful pride of life—is not of the Father but is of the world. And the world passes away and its lust but he that does the will of God abides forever."* (1 John 2.15-17)

Ambition outside of the control of God and not for His glory marks the one who exercises such ambition as a self-idolater. Selfish—Brutus type—ambition promotes idolatry because the narcissistic one seeks what will glorify himself as opposed to what will glorify God. The ambitious one proves his idolatry by bringing all within his power to secure his pleasures. The world, as they say, must revolve around him. He must control the results of his choices. He may certainly help others but he does it ultimately to help himself. He has become his own idol. He justifies all that he does and he has no room for exhortation or rebuke. This kind of ambition like an ocean tsunami can eventually consume the pursuer and wipe out everything in its grasp: family, friends, job, wealth, health.

Our ambition must have a motive that leads to a result that pleases Him. Such non-destructive ambition leaves the results or outcomes to God and grants us the liberating privilege of faithfulness. But, how often do we frame a decision as to whether it will please God? What pleases God brings glory to Him. And what pleases Him ought to please us. He saves us for His glory. He sanctifies us for His glory. Thus we must serve for His glory. Gaining the added worth of ambition for God comes as part of trusting Jesus Christ, His Son.

16

The Added Worth of Stewardship

"Christianity is not a way to do certain things.
It is a certain way to do all things."
MARY CROWLEY, FOUNDER OF MARY K. COSMETICS

"Our fruit grows up on other people's trees."
ROBERT BUFORD, HALF-TIME AUTHOR

"The works of monks and priests, however holy and arduous they be, do not differ one whit in the sight of God from the works of the rustic laborer in the field or the woman going about her household tasks, but that all works are measured before God by faith alone..."
MARTIN LUTHER, 16TH CENTURY PROTESTANT REFORMER

As we have mentioned, the Christian message has been mostly misunderstood in what it offers to the follower of Jesus. Trusting in Jesus takes care of you when you die and we should have no doubt about that. But, until we see Him in all His glory, He expects us to serve Him and to do it by His ability. The previous section on ambition reminded us that no Christian should see faith in Jesus as only a "Get out of Hell" and "Go to Heaven" card when you die. Jesus wants us to enjoy Him now and to exercise our ambition in the stewardships that He has given us. Simply put, stewardships come in two categories: those that every saint possesses and those which only certain saints possess.

What stewardships does every saint possess?

Every saint receives the stewardship of an *ambassador*. Throughout the world each nation represents itself in a variety of ways. It exports its products, its ideas, its culture and even its people. Its chief means to represent itself politically in another country comes through the representation by an embassy. At an overseas embassy, the government leaves a variety of workers. At any embassy, you might find two or three representatives of the armed forces of that nation. You might find secretaries, clerks, trained cultural analysts and probably intelligence specialists. You would certainly find one important person, the one who supervises the whole of the operation. That person would be the *chargé de faire* or the ambassador.

The ambassador represents his nation. In some cases, when the ambassador speaks, others hear him as having the weight and authority of his country. He holds a very important position as the representative overseas of his monarch, prime minister or president. However, even a powerful nation with many resources and many embassies and ambassadors cannot represent itself in every country in every place in the world.

In contrast, God has His ambassadors everywhere. Even in nations where dictators rule, God has put His representatives. As His representatives, we have the privilege to represent Him as conduits of His gospel as His ambassadors. We have the spiritual and not political privilege to communicate in truth and in love God's ministry of reconciliation. When He opens the door, the redeeming Lord has obligated his redeemed ones to speak about the identity of Jesus and about the work of Jesus. "Therefore, we are ambassadors for Christ as though God were pleading through us, we beg you on behalf of Christ, 'be reconciled to God.'" (2 Corinthians 5.20)

Every saint receives the stewardship of a *priest*. Most of us may think about the priest as someone who wears robes or some sort of ecclesiastical markings such as a collar. Those who wear robes and receive remuneration for their service we call clergy and those who don't wear robes or receive remuneration we call laity. Every saint has the added worth of being a priest.

The apostle Peter reminded the saints that we "are being built up as a spiritual house for a holy priesthood, to offer up spiritual sacrifices acceptable to God through Jesus Christ." (1 Peter 2.5) We cannot and do not have to offer animal sacrifices as God demanded of Israel as a temporary covering of sins until Christ offered His effectual sacrifice. When it comes to our sacrifice it certainly means a commitment to obey Christ and to follow Him. We are exhorted to present our bodies as a "living, holy and well-pleasing sacrifice to God which is your logical service." (Romans 12.1)

The apostle Paul exhorts the saints "to present your bodies." The word "present" carries the idea of "being ready." God wants us to keep on "being ready" to worship Him by offering our lives to the Body and to the world. Many have even lost their lives in being ready to serve Him.

A logical or reasonable service means a thoughtful choice to engage in our stewardships and exercise our responsibility. When you go to the hospital and visit an ill friend, you might hold their hand and pray with them that they might be healed or comforted in their suffering. In that example, you act as a priest because you represent God to that person and because you can intercede through Christ for them. When you pray in your private moments to God in thanksgiving and in intercession for yourself or for others, then you act in your added worth of being a priest.

Every saint has the added worth of *disciple-maker*. When Jesus left some parting words with his disciples, he spoke to us all who follow Him with these words, "As you go, make disciples of all nations …" (Matthew 28.19) Anyone who follows Jesus has the privilege of training or equipping others to follow Jesus. Today, this phrase also takes on the synonymous name of mentoring or coaching.

This added worth of discipleship for the saint/heir comes together from the streams of relationship and of revelation. We must develop a desire for His Word and the practice of studying His Word. We must also develop relationships with fellow saints who have traveled ahead of us in maturity and lag behind us in immaturity. Both of these streams ought to challenge us to get to know the

One who has saved us and be content with His work in us to provide for our needs and not just our wants.

In their book *Layman, Look Up! God Has a Place for You*, the authors Walt Henrichsen and the late Bill Garrison argue for a matrix of discipleship in growing up those who follow Jesus. Everyone who has experienced the rewards of discipling others or the joy of being discipled understands what Henrichsen and Garrison mean by a matrix. As they say, those who grow up to follow Jesus "have been the *product of a variety of ministries*." [Their italics] All these varieties of ministries exist in the church, the whole Body of Christ. For example, one saint could trace his life as a Christian in this way.

He begins his life in Christ under the tutelage of a Methodist pastor, continues in the Army with a military chaplain, later meets with a Navigator, and evangelizes along the way with a fellow Young Life leader and then sponsors the youth gatherings at an independent Bible fellowship. Throughout the life of a saint, those in the Body, the church, have contributed to the development of those who come to Christ.

A saint matures because many other saints along the way have marked his life. Garrison and Henrichsen summarize it in this way, "The church cannot be defined as one individual group or influence, but the totality of influences [that is] brought to bear by the Holy Spirit in helping a man or woman become a functioning disciple."

We may neglect this privilege of disciple-making for a variety of reasons. First, we may suffer from the wrongful thinking that the paid clergy and not the rest of us have the job of building disciples. Second, the culture has infected the church with a celebrity mentality. Those with public gifts or those who serve in far-away or strategic locations may receive undue elevation by others. Such unnatural adoration may discourage the rest of us from considering that God has a place where only we can go and serve.

And no matter our discouragement or lack of public affirmation, we cannot disparage and we ought not to envy those who have such public allegiance and well-known names.

God is in charge and we are not; it is His business and not our business as He lifts up one and puts down another.

Sometimes, we fail to make disciples because of what we think that we lack. In other words, the lack of formal academic education such as seminary or Bible school can give the saint a reticence to go and disciple others. Faithfulness and not credentials or venue ought to encourage the saint to look for opportunities to train others. We may fail to disciple others because we stop when we see little visible results in the lives of those whom we equip. Worst of all, we may fail to start because of slothfulness or just plain lack of misunderstanding about this stewardship. Nonetheless, if He has commanded, He can grant us the ability to accomplish what He desires.

How do stewardships differ among the saints?

Every saint has the stewardship of *gifts* but not every saint has the same gift. The apostle made that clear when he said, "There are different gifts but the same Spirit." (1 Corinthians 12.4) Here the apostle refers to the internal spiritual gifts or spiritual abilities that God has given to every saint. At least four passages list the spiritual gifts that God has given. The first passage refers to the gifts in the context of seeing Christ as a victor. When Christ ascended and returned to His heavenly abode, He gave gifts to His followers. These gifts of Christ are listed in Ephesians 4.8-13 and usually speak of the whole person as the gift: apostles, prophets, evangelists and pastor-teachers. While every saint is called to discipleship, these gifted saints are specifically called to equip the saints.

Two passages refer to the gifts as gifts of the Spirit. We usually refer to these gifts as the *charismatic* gifts because the New Testament Greek word used for the gift is *charis* or grace. You find the lists in 1 Corinthians 12: 4-11, Romans 12.6-8. People differ over the exact number of the gifts, the use of the gifts and the limit in time of the gifts. The verses in Romans list the following: prophecy, service, teaching, exhortation, material giving, leadership, and mercy. The verses in First Corinthians list: practical wisdom, knowledge, faith, healings, miracles, prophecy, discernment, languages (commonly called tongues), interpretation of languages. This writer takes the view that the sign gifts of miracles, languages and healings have ceased.

In the final passage the apostle Peter puts all the gifts into two categories: speaking and serving. Peter emphasizes the gifting of every person when he says, "as each one has received a gift, employ it..." (1 Peter 4.10) He also reminds the readers of what the apostle Paul had said to the church at Corinth. God has given these gifts of grace so that they can be used for the common good among the saints. The gifts have not been given to give greater status to one over another or to bring pride to one who has a more prominent gift than another. It appears that Peter classifies all the gifts according to their function. The apostle Paul, on the other hand, lists specific gifts in his passages.

> *"Just as each one has received a gift of grace for one another go serve as good stewards of the diverse grace of God."* (1 Peter 4.10)

Like all stewardships, this added worth of gifts God has given that we may serve as He has chosen for His glory. God gave all the gifts for the common good and He gave them as He saw fit to give them. Ambition has His glory as the motive; faithfulness in stewardships has the common good as a purpose.

What motivates us?

British General Charles "Chinese" Gordon (1830-1885) had a distinguished military career that included fighting in the Crimean War and in leading troops mainly composed of Chinese in the Taiping rebellion in Shanghai in 1842. The king of Ethiopia threatened to take the life of Gordon once but declined after Gordon said, "I am always ready to die." The king could only depart and say, "Then my power has no terrors over you."

Later, Gordon and all the defenders perish in a fierce fight in his defense of Khartoum to save the lives of hundreds who lived there. Os Guinness summarizes the philosophy of the faith of Gordon in Christ, "I live before the

Audience of One. Before others I have nothing to prove, nothing to love."

That pretty much explains humility and the motivation to be responsible in our stewardships. If I am on stage, only God sits in the audience. I must speak and act for His benefit, for His glory, for His reward. He directs the play of all our lives. More than that, He has paid for and has provided a Spirit enabled performance. He expects to get His due. It cannot get simpler than that.

What captures all our responsibilities?

The unduly maligned Puritans are credited with describing the calling of a Christian as "by God, to God, and for God." In terms of all that we do, He deserves the credit and the glory for His work in us. The Puritans also said that in regard to His children, God calls "everyone, everywhere, in everything." In terms of "everything," all of life for the saint belongs to God and all that we do we ought to do for Him. In terms of "everyone," while He calls every saint to serve in a stewardship, He does not call every saint to serve in the same place or in the same way. In terms of "everywhere," the apologist Francis Schaeffer summarized calling like this, "... in God's sight there are no little places and no little people."

> "*... work out your salvation because it is God who is at work in you both to will and work for His good pleasure.*" (Philippians 4.12, 13)

"For not from the east or from the west and not from the wilderness comes lifting up but it is God who judges by putting down one and lifting up another." (Psalm 75.6, 7)

17

The Added Worth of Love

That British foursome said it musically years ago with this line, "All you need is love." Another song lyric took the same tact, "What the world needs now is love." While John Lennon could write about love, he also did not care much for Jesus, the epitome of love. Although he apparently apologized before his murder in 1980, he once claimed that the Beatles were more popular than Jesus. In a certain way these lyrics hold the truth. People do need love and most people want to be loved. But, how do we know when we are acting in love or others are acting in love toward us? Without a definition of love, how can we exercise a true and beneficial love?

Love sometimes belies an acceptable and exact definition because of the diversity of definitions. The English language does not help since it fails us in regard to a definition because the word love must be stretched to capture so many meanings. One can say, "I love chocolate" and later in the same breath say, "I love my dog" or "I love my wife." Certainly the love of chocolate and the love of an animal cannot be the same as the love of a woman. In some ways, they are the same since each contains some degree of commitment or desire. Nonetheless, an understanding of people's pursuit of love requires more discussion about the definition of love because we may not truly understand the nature of love. More importantly, we may think that we are acting in love when we are only acting in self-interest.

The ancients spoke more precisely than those of us who speak the so-called King's English. The Greeks had at least four different words to define love. If you loved someone or something in an *Eros* way, then you would seek to consume the thing or person that you love. Thus, a chocoholic could not wait to crunch down that confection. Or, a young man may only love a young woman in the *Eros* sense just to satisfy his uncontrolled, physical needs. Both would fit the idea of *Eros. Eros* compels itself to seek satisfaction in the object of its pursuit. Lust might work at times as a synonym for *Eros.*

If you love someone in a *Storge'* way, you may be a child who respects his parents or even an animal such as a dog that loves his master. Devotion or affection might work as synonyms for this kind of love. If you loved someone in a *Phileo* way, you would be seen as a friend and not suffocating or possessive such as *Eros* or as weak or casual as *Storge'*. Whether or not they really do love one another, those who live in Philadelphia live in a city whose name means "brotherly love." This kind of *Phileo* love would include hospitality, care and concern for others.

The final love of *Agape* describes a love of sacrifice. This kind of love a soldier or a fireman must have in order to save others. Only this kind of love would cause a person to race into a burning building or a raging battle when others may be fleeing. One who has *Agape* love will not only lay down his life to save another but has a compulsion to do it. In terms of others, he will act for the common good as God defines that common good. This love marks the highest kind of love.

The noted classics professor C. S. Lewis summarized love best for our discussion. He observed that the practical definition of love really comes down to two kinds of love: *need-love* and *gift-love*. These two kinds of love reflect the two different poles of love. On the one end, need-love focuses solely upon "taking." A person will love something or someone if the object of love meets a need in that lover's life. Need-love comes with conditions with that object of love. In need-love, if the object of love meets the demands of the lover, then the lover will give the object his love. In the process, however, the object will be consumed or controlled or manipulated. Worst yet, such love could lead to hate or abuse. Commonly this love so acts that the object of love must give back to the lover. Many practice this kind of conditional love.

In contrast, gift-love focuses solely upon "giving." This altruistic sort of love expects to receive no return from the object upon which the love is bestowed. This love comes as a gift of grace. In other words, grace means that the agape lover expects nothing from the object of love in return. Also, the lover who manifests agape gives without regard to the response of the object. This gift-love manifests its highest form when the lover lays down his life for the rescue of the beloved. When a fireman rushes into a burning building, he certainly deserves thanks but we expect him to do that and do not consider it out of the ordinary. When an untrained civilian rushes into a burning building to save a person, we may call it extraordinary because we do not expect an ordinary and untrained person to be so reckless. Yet, both manifested love.

This no-strings-attached kind of love may be difficult to practice. But, we can love in such a beneficial way and act as givers for two reasons. First, the incarnation and the shed blood of God upon the cross for sins act as a model for us who follow Jesus. Additionally, the Spirit of God now indwells every saint so that each one of us can be givers and manifest agape love. Unconditional love speaks of maturity in the lover and the highest form of nobility in humans.

When Paul the apostle went to Macedonia to evangelize the Thessalonians, he spoke of this kind of gift love. He and his team spent a very short time there as the book of Acts records in Chapter 17. This brevity of time failed to prevent the apostle and his partners from practicing gift-love toward those at Thessalonica.

He spoke in this way about love in terms of others. The apostle did not just give a message to them but he gave the model of love by being with them. He spoke and he acted with love.

> *"Since we cared so much for you, we were well-pleased to share with you not only our Gospel but our very lives because you had become beloved [agapatos] to us."* (1 Thessalonians 2.8)

18

The Added Worth of Peace

"Imagine all the people living life in peace"
JOHN LENNON

"All we are saying is give peace a chance.
All we are saying is give peace a chance."
JOHN LENNON

On January 6, 2008, the New York Times ran a one page notice. Only two words in large font took the center place on the page: "IMAGINE PEACE." The words "Love, Yoko" marked the bottom of the page. Many of us have heard what her late husband had written about peace in two different songs whose excerpts appear above. These lyrics personify peace and speak as if this entity of peace has never had a chance. His definition of peace in life comes down to a mental visualization that will bring everyone together no matter the race, the nationality and, most importantly, the religion or as he said, the "isms."

In spite of Yoko's wish, peace has little chance in a world like ours. Hostility, anger, malice, hatred—all such attitudes reflect and contribute to a predisposition for conflict. Two great wars molded the Twentieth Century. At the conclusion of those great and awful World Wars, the peoples of the liberated nations spontaneously went to the streets to express their joy through dancing, singing, hugging and kissing. Unfortunately, for many, that jubilation lived a short life as more wars followed as nations re-shifted to gain control of other nations. After World War 1, the victorious leaders proclaimed that the war was a "war to end all wars." World War II disproved that as did the wars in Korea and Vietnam.

Leaders of nations have regularly traded tractors for tanks and turned ploughshares into swords and drafted farmers to be soldiers. This new century continues to have the world at war although the venues may be more localized or unexpected in an era of global terrorism.

In these conflicts, millions have lost their lives in combat, in pogroms [purposed annihilation of particular groups by government rulers] such as the Holocaust and in indiscriminate murders and/or persecutions of civilian bystanders. The wars on earth mask the underlying war—the war in people's hearts. The enemy is not another nation or another people; the enemy is us. When we speak of global peace among peoples of the world and yet deny the call to have peace with God, our deceit buries the bellicose seed that will eventually again bear the poisonous fruit of war. Self-deceit promotes our unnatural independence and contributes to a misunderstanding about the origin of peace.

The enemy that we as the human race oppose we cannot see: the Creator of the universe. By our wickedness of independence and native bent toward evil, we say, as a human race, "Not Thy will be done but my will be done."

This fruit of pride that causes local and global war comes from a seed of self-willfulness.

As His enemy, the human race sits in the camp of the infernal one who has opposed God almost from the beginning. This prince of pride even opposed God before the creation of the human race. Although he and his demonic followers will eventually experience the judgment of God, they contribute to the war among us humans. Until global peace does come, war rages as it takes a variety of expressions worldwide: famine, pestilence, starvation, massacres.

We certainly grow tired and do not want to talk about such ugliness of conflict that can be found anytime in the media in a twenty-four hour seven days a week news cycle.

In the quiet moments where contemplation banishes busyness, we sense within ourselves that we long for peace not just for ourselves but for others.

How does the added worth of peace come to the friend of God?

> *"Thus, since we have been justified by faith, we have peace with God through our Lord Jesus Christ."* (Romans 5.1)

Some historian in the industry of greeting cards could know when the jolly man in the red suit that Coca-Cola promoted replaced the nativity scene of the baby Jesus with Mary and Joseph plus the shepherds. In recent holidays of Christmas celebration, a menagerie of animals, snowy scenes and cartoon characters have joined the different portraits of St. Nicholas. Even the message has evolved into inane, vague phrases or words that allude to biblical passages such as: "Happy Holidays," "Peace on Earth," "All the Joy of the Season."

On that night of the Messiah's birth, the shepherds whom Israel considered unclean or even outcast heard a different, precise and clear Christmas greeting.

> *"Glory to God in the highest and on earth andpeace among men of good pleasure."* (Luke 2.14)

Different versions translate "good pleasure" [NT Greek *eudokias*] in this way: "with whom He is pleased" (NET Bible; NASB 95); "good pleasure in men" (1890 Darby Bible); "to those in whom His favor rests" (NIV); "good will toward men" (KJV) and "men of good will."(Douay-Rheims Bible). In terms of the world-view of this presentation, the NIV best expresses the meaning. Only those men and women upon whom God's favor rests can find peace both now and forever.

In order to have even a chance of true and continuing personal peace, you must have the favor of God. The favor or grace of God comes when the Prince of Peace, the Lord Jesus Christ, rules in your life. That begins with your justification. Friendship with God does not necessarily give His friend a pass from the sufferings of wars in the world or crimes on the street or even the sufferings of so-called natural disasters. Earthly suffering will come but the eternal war has ended. God's friend has peace with

God because He has terminated the war with those who surrender to Him. That declaration of peace with Him creates and sustains personal peace because of His purchase when He "made peace through the blood of his cross..." (Colossians 1.20)

How does the added worth of peace work in tragedy?

Scripture reports one particular family in the nation of Israel that Jesus loved: Mary, Martha and their brother Lazarus. When Lazarus fell ill and was dying, the sisters sent for Jesus to come to heal him. Jesus declined to hurry back to their home in Bethany and Lazarus died. Jesus gave His reason for that delay, "This sickness is not unto death, but for the glory of God that the Son of God might be glorified by it." (John 11.4) In spite of his love for them, Jesus delayed so that He would prove Himself as the Messiah by raising Lazarus from the dead.

Who can have peace when a loved one dies? When Jesus delayed himself from our point of view and arrived too late to heal Lazarus, Martha, the first sister to greet Jesus, told Jesus that His presence would have saved her brother. In spite of her grief, Martha could have peace because she knew Jesus and the faith of her brother, "I know that he shall rise again in the resurrection in the last day." (John 11.24) After Martha proclaimed her faith in Jesus publicly, she went to speak privately to Mary, her sister who had not yet seen Jesus.

As Jesus approached her house, Mary went out, greeted him and bowed down and spoke just as her sister had spoken to Jesus, "If you had been here, my brother would not have died." (John 11.32) John comments briefly but effectively on the deep and intensely troubled feelings of Jesus and then writes, "Jesus wept." (John 11.35) As he approached the tomb of Lazarus to remove the stone, Martha had resigned herself to resurrection of her brother in the future and not then. She could not imagine an immediate resurrection and opposed the removal of the stone on her brother's tomb, "Lord, by this time there will be a bad smell because he has been dead four days." (John 11.39)

Jesus raised Lazarus. That miracle and the resumed earthly life of Lazarus would now serve as proof of Jesus as the Messiah. His life would also be endangered as the religious leaders would seek to kill Lazarus as well as Jesus.

Although the passage fails to mention the concept of peace, the actions of Martha suggest that she had such an internal contentment that we call peace. This peace did not deny her the grief and the expressed emotion over the loss of her beloved brother. Although Jesus knew of the imminent resurrection of Lazarus, he had grief in spite of the peace because He knew that He could raise Lazarus. This sense of settleness for Martha in the midst of tragedy rested on her relationship to Jesus and her commitment to his words. Jesus had said to her,

> *"I am the resurrection and the life; the one who believes in me shall live [eternally] even if he dies [physically]."* (John 11.25)

Internal peace derives its existence from a commitment to Him and His word. When a person trusts Christ, the Savior now governs the saint. The friends of God must make a choice to depend upon Him. As Isaiah says in 9.7: "Of his government and peace there shall be no end…" Government and peace go together. You can have personal peace when He rules over your life. While we may not understand all that He does or permits, we rest in the comfort that "God is not a God of confusion but of peace…" (1 Corinthians 14.33) We can have peace because we know that He works for the good of His children.

We have such a worm's eye view of life and so we get stuck in the moment and awfulness of an event. He has a bird's eye view of all and knows the whole of it all. He thus rules in a way that we cannot understand. So, we must guard ourselves against trying to understand where we have no permission to understand. We can live however in the confidence that he will eventually establish peace and that he will judge righteously. Peace comes when we recognize and accept such doings by Him.

> *"And we know that to those that love God all things work together for good, to those who are the called according to His purpose."* (Romans 8.28)

On the other hand, sometimes in the midst of tragedy or conflict, well-meaning but misguided wannabe counselor friends will quote 1 Thessalonians 5.18: "In everything give thanks for this is the will of God in Christ Jesus for you."

They would see the way to peace as "Thank God for the tragedy." This misplaced translation has little merit. It suggests that evil has a place in our lives. We cannot escape pain or tragedy but the sovereign Lord does not act in an evil way. God stands as the object of our thanksgiving. We thank God that He controls.

Mary and Martha voiced their questions to Jesus. Mary and Martha expressed their deepest hurt to Jesus over the loss of their brother. Their conviction that this Messiah would raise up their brother eventually resulted in peace for them. That peace erupted into unbelievable joy when their brother rose up and struggled to be freed from his earthly burial clothes.

What calms our hearts?

"When peace like a river attendeth my way
When sorrows like sea billows roll Whatever my lot
Thou hast taught me to say,
'It is well; it is well with my soul!"

Horatio G. Spafford (1828-1888)

Horatio Spafford, attorney and successful real estate investor, had three almost contemporaneous major tragedies that provided the genesis of the well-known song whose one verse appears above. As an evangelical Christian in his day, he knew well the evangelist and educator Dwight Moody and supported him in his efforts of his Gospel work. Spafford's house also acted as an evangelical epicenter to provide a meeting place such as for those who met to end slavery or alcohol sales in America. In 1870, his four-year-old son died of scarlet fever. In 1871, the Great Chicago Fire wiped out almost all of his income. In spite of these tragedies of loss of a son and real estate holdings, he and his wife ministered to the homeless which numbered about 90,000 after the fire.

In November, 1873, he decided to take his family and join Moody and Ira Sankey, Moody's song leader, on a crusade in Great Britain that would make Moody and Sankey household names in Great Britain. A business emergency caused Spafford to miss his ship but he sent his family ahead on the ship *Ville Du Havre*. It collided with another ship halfway across the Atlantic. All four of his daughters died. When Anna Spafford reached Great Britain, she sent a telegram from Wales to her husband with these words, "Saved alone. What shall I do?" Certainly grief stricken, Spafford immediately sailed for Wales. He later wrote, "On Thursday last we passed over the spot where she went down, in mid-ocean, the waters three miles deep. But I do not think of our dear ones there. They are safe, folded, the dear lambs." In his cabin, he penned the well-known hymn *It is Well with My Soul* that expressed his inner peace about his loss.

Like Job, God gave Anna and Horatio more children. In spite of their loss, he also contended with those in his local church who wondered what sin he had committed to suffer such discipline by God. Years later, their daughter would say, "Father became convinced that God was kind and that he would see his children again in heaven. This thought calmed his heart, but it was to bring Father into open conflict with what was then the Christian world...

To Father, this was a passing through the 'valley of the shadow of death,' but his faith came through triumphant and strong."

In 1881, they moved to Jerusalem to establish a Christian community as an evangelistic outreach through medical services. They never returned to live in America and eventually saw conversions in the Arab community.

Suffering has its place in all our lives and others may think that they know the cause of our suffering. We must remember that Jesus has gone ahead of us and guarantees an eventual escape from suffering at our resurrection. Like Horatio and Anna, we keep looking to Jesus and doing His work so that He receives the glory.

How does the friend of God find daily peace?

> *"Be anxious for nothing but in all things by prayer and supplication with thanksgiving let your requests be known to God and the peace of God which passes all understanding shall guard your hearts and minds in Christ Jesus."* (Philippians 4.6, 7)

Inner peace means trust in His unconditional love. The sinner comes to God through Christ the Savior in weakness. To live in weakness in dependence upon Christ continues to mark out the Christian life. "My grace is sufficient for you for [My] power is perfected in weakness." (2 Corinthians 12.9)

Our weakness also extends to our knowledge. We cannot know everything and we cannot know for sure unless He has revealed it in His Word. We can certainly always know that He does have purpose and knows what He is doing. We must attend to our business while He attends to His.

In Galatians 5.22, 23, the apostle Paul lists the virtues of the saint; he calls these nine virtues the fruit of the Spirit. They include: love, joy, peace, patience, kindness, goodness, faithfulness, meekness, and self-control. This fruit like all virtues speaks of that which dwells within a person. Although this fruit has a supernatural enabling, the manifestation of peace or any aspect of the fruit requires diligence. It means trusting the living Lord who has brought peace to you by ending the war. On the other hand, it means diligence to learn his Word that informs you and enables you to live out a life in Christ.

With just a few exceptions, the sun provides the energy for organisms to fuel their activities. Botanists call this process photosynthesis whose etymology includes two Greek words: *photos* [light] and *syntithenai* [to put together]. This analogy illustrates the challenge of every Christian in the process that we could call *logos-synthesis* where the word [*logos*—His Word] by His Holy Spirit enters our lives so that we may live out this life in Christ. The friend of God must choose to study His Word so as to know Him and to know our response to His work in the world. Without the sun, organisms cannot develop. Without His Word, the saints cannot develop; we must take seriously His communication to us if we want growth let alone peace. He acts sovereignly; the saints must act responsibly.

"But, I say, walk by the Spirit and do not carry out the deeds of the flesh." (Galatians 5.16)

"Let the word of Christ dwell in you all richly..." (Colossians 2.16a)

Can we have peace with others?

Younger evangelicals like to plant churches not just overseas but here and especially in urban areas. Prior to their endeavors, others planted churches. As the joke goes, most church plants of years ago resulted from church splits. Even a small community can have a 1st, 2nd or even a 3rd Baptist or Presbyterian in a community. As a seminary professor once said, "If you could find the perfect local church, do not join it. If you do, it will be imperfect." Friends of God have conflicts with one another and conflict threatens personal peace.

Most conflicts ought not to be. Over thirty years ago, the late Joe Aldrich wrote *Life-Style Evangelism.* Joe's book explains a practical and successful philosophy of ministry to represent the gospel of Jesus beyond the walls of the local congregation. In Chapter Two, he introduces the reader to the *professional* weaker brother. This person has developed a view of sanctification that rests on tradition and culture and not necessarily Scripture. He could be the person who would have condemned Jesus for speaking to a Samaritan woman.

This person may also "make war" with other saints over issues that other saints consider unimportant. In religious circles, two phrases explain how others may gather in peace: *closed hand* and *open hand*. Every local congregation has its beliefs that fit into either one of these two categories. For example, the gospel of Jesus as explained in 1 Corinthians 15 fits into the closed hand category. It cannot be modified without doing damage to the fellowship. The same congregation might fit mode of baptism into the open hand category. It could permit baptism by sprinkling, pouring or immersion. More issues such as the mode of worship would fit into this discussion of commitment to others in a local congregation.

The professional weaker brother considers and confronts anyone who opposes his view as sinful or wrong. This particular problem may seem small until you find yourself confronted by those who every Sunday will query you as to the absence of a tie on your shirt. A deacon could demand that a man must only wear a black or brown suit but not a blazer sans tie to serve the Lord's Table.

The harder conflict concerns those who have wronged you or you have wronged. The wrong could come in a variety of venues. The worst war among the friends of God comes in the venue of morality. The culture of America today permits behavior that clearly opposes Scripture. How do you resolve the war and gain peace with a person who must be confronted over immorality? Do we ignore others who have conflict with us? Or do we just regard others who go to war against us as part of the things of an ongoing difficult day on a yet unredeemed earth?

Some of us will escape the kinds of people who take away our peace. Paul and Barnabas broke peace in a sharp conflict over the desertion of John Mark to the apostolic work. Barnabas escaped that conflict so that it never escalated into a war. Barnabas took his nephew [cousin?] John Mark with him for apostolic work; Paul began a new team with Silas. (Acts 15.36-41) Barnabas apparently at that moment forgave John Mark and Paul; much later did Paul forgive John Mark. (2 Timothy 4.11) [This added worth of forgiveness will be discussed more in the next chapter.]

Some imperatives help us in our conflict with others:

1. Glorify God. (1 Corinthians 10.31)
2. Get the log out of your eye. (1 Corinthians 7.5)
3. Gently restore. (Galatians 6.1)
4. Go and be reconciled. (Matthew 5.24)

In spite of all your efforts, you may not have peace with others. They may wage war with you because you refused to change over their penchant for an *open hand* issue. They may wage war with you because you confronted them over their immoral behavior. They may even wage a cold war with you because they have heard gossip about you.

Nevertheless, God has called us to peace. That definitely means an end to the war with Him. That calling to peace undergirds the call to daily Spirit-enabled personal inner peace. Sadly, too many times we learn to live in peace in spite of others' wars against us.

> *"As near as it is possible with you, be at peace with all men."* (Romans 12.18)

When will peace finally have a chance?

> *"Let the peace of Christ rule over your hearts into which also you were called in one body and give thanks."* (Colossians 3.13)

We live in a world without peace but a Christian abides in the best peace of all; the friend of God has peace with God. God has chased down these human combatants whom He now calls friends, reached down toward them and declared an armistice, an armistice that comes with reparations of added worth and eventual rewards. Instead of an old life of independence, the friend of God has a new life of dependence on Him.

We can have no national or global peace until all hearts have changed. As His saints, we know that cannot happen now. In the meantime, we are called to work on our own personal peace. We must look to Jesus to do that.

> *"Fixing our eyes on Jesus, the pioneer and perfecter of our faith, who for the joy that was set before Him endured the cross, despising the shame, and sat down at the right hand of the throne of God."* (Hebrews 12.2)

The joy of Jesus found its source in His eventual enthronement in peace with and beside His Father. We may not be able to have a precise definition for peace but we can know the cause of it.

For the world as a whole to have true peace, the Prince of Peace must rule on earth. To have a chance of true and continuing personal peace, you must have the favor of God. You must remember that He knows you and what you are facing. Until Jesus returns, those who truly know the Prince must turn to Him in weakness and in faith to have personal peace.

19

The Added Worth of Forgiveness

One event characterizes the plight of the Jews in recent history: the Holocaust. To the Jews this national tragedy stands out in their modern history as a motivation for survival and as a haunting reminder for anyone about the love and power of God. Out of that pogrom came a survivor, Simon Wiesenthal, (1908 - 2005), who made it his life's vocation to find Nazis who had been responsible for such wickedness. He practiced his vocation quite successfully.

His incarceration led to an unresolved dilemma later in life about this issue of forgiveness. In 1969, when he could no longer escape the pain which he felt due to one memorable and haunting incident in his unwarranted incarceration during World War II, he writes a book on one specific experience. He asks others to answer the question that a dying soldier had asked him, "Will you forgive me for what I have done?" [Here the soldier refers to the Jews that he and others had murdered when they secured a building with Jews inside and set fire to it.]

In *The Sunflower,* Wiesenthal sets the stage as he describes his daily march with the other prisoners to work.

Every day they would pass by his old Technical School which the Nazis had converted into an infirmary and the graveyard where the Nazis buried their comrades in arms. At the cemetery, a sunflower would be planted on the grave of every German soldier. Wiesenthal envied the dead soldiers because sunflowers decorated their graves and, from Simon's point of view, connected them yet to the living world. Wiesenthal reckoned that even in death the Nazis remained superior to the Jews. If he died at the Nazi murderers' hands, no flower would mark his grave. He would join others in a large unmarked mass grave. For many Jews, to remember the dead does, in some way, keep them alive.

One evening, a guard brought Simon to the infirmary and a nurse secreted him into the infirmary beside his camp and to a bed where a German soldier lay dying. This soldier wanted to make amends for the atrocities which he had committed against Jews. He wanted to confess his sins to a Jew. The well-bandaged and dying soldier grabbed the hand of Simon, explained his heinous deed and asked, "Will you forgive me for what I have done?" Simon walked away and did not say anything. Eventually he felt so guilty about his choice not to forgive that he went and found the mother of the soldier after the war.

Wiesenthal acknowledges that the dying SS soldier had true repentance. The soldier spoke of confession so that he might be clean when he died. Wiesenthal even concedes that the "murderous ideology" had made the SS soldier a murderer. Nonetheless, Simon thought that if the soldier had "really rediscovered his faith in Christianity," why would he not confess to a priest? He further thinks, "What should I have done?"

Wiesenthal sent this narrative to 46 highly respected individuals in the world and asked them the question, "Should I have forgiven the soldier?" "Would you have forgiven the soldier?" "What would you have done?" He published the results of their responses in the second half of *The Sunflower*.

How does the saint work with forgiveness?

We may not suffer as Simon and his fellow Jews suffered but we must wrestle with the question of forgiveness. How ought the saint to respond to such a question? The early childhood education primer used to contain the words, "I am sorry." The young toddler sees the world within his scope as solely his world. He won't let anyone command him or oppose his desires. The entry of another toddler into his space with the same intent toward the same toy creates an impasse with a ready-made invitation for both to learn. The mature parent now teaches the toddlers what must be a mainstay in all of life: conflict resolution. They now must say those words of release—"I am sorry"—to resolve the conflict.

Those three words of "I am sorry" fail to expose the foundation of the problem. True sorrow spawns a plea for forgiveness by the offender; however, the choice to forgive rests with the offended party. In an absolute sense, although the offender proffers the plea, the offended one has the sole right to respond. Wiesenthal recognizes the issue when he writes later in the book, "Without forgiveness, there is no future." If Simon had forgiven the soldier, would Simon have gained a sense of release, a sense of freedom?

How do sinners gain forgiveness?

Actions do have consequences. Sins have consequences that keep us from being connected to others and certainly from being connected to God. A Christian world-view built upon the Bible certainly sees all people as equal before God in at least two respects:

Men and women have offended God, their Creator.

Men and women need forgiveness from God, the Redeemer.

Unresolved conflict reaps a harvest of resentment, bitterness, and even hatred toward others. Those who lack forgiveness from others and/or have been genuinely offended may be dominated by anger, guilt and even ill health. If you suffer the death of a relationship on earth by withholding love or repentance, you may just move on and not try to resurrect the connection. The pain may be too great or so you think. The passing of a lot of time may not make forgiveness any easier for those in conflict whether they play the role of the offended one or the role of the offender.

Not until sixty years after the Allies invaded Normandy on D-Day did any representative of the Republic of Germany attend the Allied commemoration of those who gave their lives to liberate Europe from the Nazis. It took that long to bring enough mutual forgiveness for previous enemies to meet although Europe had already united its continental nations on economic issues.

Consider the consequences beyond this life if you fail to pinpoint and consider seriously the heavenly conflict as the larger and unseen cause of the earthly conflict. Without forgiveness from God, a person cannot resolve the conflict with Heaven. Without forgiveness from God, a person may not be able to resolve the conflict between him and someone else. A lack of God's forgiveness contributes to earthly immaturity and eternal loneliness.

The murdering burdens of guilt and condemnation within a conscience confirm conflict. Only the application of forgiveness can resolve the conflict and liberate a person from true guilt and eternal condemnation. Only the atonement of Christ can make the possibility of forgiveness available. On the basis of Christ's death alone, God has forgiven those who have trusted His Son and lifted the burden of sin's guilt by removing His wrath and extracting His new friend from the camp of the enemy.

How do sinners gain forgiveness?

This standing of forgiveness has daily application. As imperfect friends of God, we yet offend Him maybe not always on a daily basis but it happens. God has given His friends ongoing, never-ending opportunities for the forgiveness that results from momentary or seasonal lapses of displeasing Him or harming others. When the friend of God discovers through conviction or discipline that he needs forgiveness, God is ready to receive the confession that brings forgiveness.

Friends on earth may not always forgive us and continue to carry grudges. In contrast, God will always forgive His friends immediately and regularly. No time has to pass to come regularly to Him for forgiveness. Even if much time has passed since the offense, God still stands ready to forgive. Gaining the added worth of the forgiveness of God comes as part of trusting Jesus Christ, His Son.

> *"If we confess our sins, he is faithful and just to forgive our sins and cleanse us from all unrighteousness."* (1 John 1.9)

When does the friend of God forgive?

As odd as it may sound, a person who denies forgiveness to a truly repentant offender makes that offended one a debtor to him. To withhold forgiveness gives the offended one a chance to have some sort of power over another or even to punish that person passively by refusing resolution or reconciliation.

Jesus spoke a parable about this difficult issue of practicing forgiveness. Peter spoke for us all when he asked, "Lord, how often shall my brother sin against me and I forgive him—up to seven times? (*indefinitely?*)" (Matthew 18.22) Jesus corrected Peter by multiplying the number of times to forgive by ten. In other words, no one has the permission not to forgive. As Wiesenthal has shown in his book, following such advice proves difficult. We do not want to forgive because we want justice now. If we cannot literally physically hurt a person, we can figuratively hurt them by not forgiving them.

Jesus then gives a parable to accent how strongly Jesus thought about this issue. In the parable, a king prepares to seize the possessions of a debtor and sell everything including the debtor and his family because he owed him an astronomical amount of ten thousand talents [approximately ten million dollars]. When the king spoke the command, the slave fell down and said, "Have patience with me and I will restore everything to you." (Matthew 18.26) The king forgave him and released him from the debt. On the way home, the forgiven slave seeks out and finds another slave who owed him a debt of only one hundred denarii [approximately six thousand dollars]. The second slave falls down and asks the same question, "Have patience with me and I will restore everything to you." (Matthew 18.26) The slave whom the master had forgiven refuses to forgive the smaller debt and sends the one who owes him money to prison. Later, the king hears of the unmerciful actions of the slave whom he forgave. He has the slave brought before him, rebukes him and then sends him to be tortured.

> *"You wicked slave, all this debt I forgave you because you begged me. Is it not necessary for you not to have mercy on your fellow slave as I had mercy on you?"* (Matthew 18.32-33)

It takes humility to forgive others. An offender has already put the offended down and now the offended one must grant the offender grace in the proffer of forgiveness. Jesus expects His followers to forgive.

Somewhat commonly the media runs a story about a family who forgives a criminal who has murdered someone in their family. The commentators ask, "How is this possible?" Those who know Christ have no choice; they must forgive. Friendship with God permits the expression and actions of forgiveness.

On the other hand, forgiveness does not infer forgetting. In other words, you may forgive someone for an offense against you but you may not be able to be associated with them any longer.

Also, "taking offense" has developed a broader definition than it ought. Sometimes, adults sound quite childish when they claim others must ask forgiveness because of an offense against them. Many times the word "offense" really just means a disagreement or holding a contrastive view on some issue. Each person must search his own conscience and decide if what another has done really counts as an offense.

Earlier in the chapter on peace, we referenced the verse in Romans that suggests not all will be at peace with us in spite of all that we do. Some people may refuse to ask for forgiveness for a true offense. Others may refuse your offer of forgiveness. Both refusals produce the same result in terms of the relationships. In either case without the true experience of forgiveness, the failure to forgive or the failure to accept forgiveness means a failure in the relationship and a decline in and maybe even the death of the relationship.

> *"And be kind to one another, tenderhearted, forgiving one another, even as God in Christ forgave you."* (Ephesians 4.32)

> *"Bearing with one another, and forgiving one another, if anyone has a complaint against another; even as Christ forgave you, so you also must do."* (Colossians 3:13)

How does the friend of God offer or gain forgiveness?

You can identify a good restaurant not just by its cuisine but also by how it responds to a customer when the cuisine results in complaints from the diner. If the entrée fails to meet a person's expectations or the reputation of the restaurant, then a good restaurant will re-do the order willingly and probably offer the patron a dessert or make the entrée gratis. If the food fails completely, a good restaurant may pay for the meal.

Scripture attests to this idea. Jacob realized that he had wronged his brother Esau and on the advice of his mother immediately left. He found himself in a similarly manipulative situation where his uncle took advantage of him so that he had to remain outside of the Promised Land and in foreign territory.

After a twenty year absence, Jacob decided to return to the Promised Land. In spite of angelic assurance of God's presence and a wrestling match with the pre-incarnate

Christ, Jacob yet remained fearful. He wanted to gain favor with Esau so he sent his family, flocks and servants ahead of him to assuage the assumed anger of his brother Esau.

> *"So he [Jacob] lodged there that same night, and took what came to his hand as a present for Esau his brother."* (Genesis 32.13)

> *"But Esau ran to meet him, and embraced him, and fell on his neck and kissed him, and they wept."* (Genesis 33.4)

Jacob had an unfounded fear of facing Esau because he had yet to ask Esau for forgiveness. After all, he had stolen the birthright of Esau. When they do meet, Jacob persuades Esau to take the gifts. Esau, the wronged brother, immediately forgives Jacob and acts more like God than does Jacob who had just wrestled with God.

Readiness to forgive reflects the desires of God. Forgiveness may mean a material compensation for reconciliation. Forgiveness certainly might also mean a repayment of a debt. Jacob unfortunately saw his gifts as a bribe to win the favor of his brother rather than a payment for reconciliation and compensation. Too many friends of God borrow money from another and refuse to repay it. Instead of asking for forgiveness or repaying some of it, the borrower ignores the fellow brother and may even switch local congregations to avoid that person.

A readiness to forgive instead of a choosing to punish stands out in the parable of the Prodigal Son. (Luke 15) Jesus portrays the seeking father as the one who has the readiness to forgive. As the parable goes, the son takes his inheritance prematurely and squanders it. When he comes to his senses, he leaves his squalor and rehearses his plea for forgiveness on the way back. The son has no opportunity to speak; the father has a readiness to forgive. While he forgives without hesitation, the text fails to reveal if the son ever received any more inheritance although the son remained as a son and not as a slave.

> *"And he arose and came to his father. But when he was still a great way off, his father saw him and had compassion, and ran and fell on his neck and kissed him."* (Luke 15.20)

The older brother resented the forgiveness of the father. The father explained to the stay-at-home son the cause of celebration,

> *"It was necessary that we should make merry, and be glad: for this your brother was dead, and is alive again; and was lost, and is found."* (Luke 15.32)

Why is it difficult to forgive yourself?

A scribe once approached Jesus after he heard the debate between Jesus and the religious leaders. The scribe asked Jesus to identify the foremost commandment of all. Jesus summarized the law in this way, "Hear, O Israel, the Lord our God, the Lord is one, and you shall love the Lord your

God with all your heart, with all your soul, with all your mind, and with all your strength. And the second is, 'Love your neighbor as [you love] yourself.'" (Mark 12.28-31a)

Many of us have heard this answer that Jesus gave. We may also know that Jesus defined the neighbor in the Parable of the Good Samaritan. The Samaritan saw his neighbor as someone in need even if that someone had a different religion or ethnic background. We fail, however, to accent the latter part of the verse. We should take care of and love our neighbor just as we love ourselves no matter the unlikeness of our neighbor in comparison to us.

Some of us cannot forgive ourselves because we really do not love ourselves. We do not speak here of some sort of cultural narcissism where we spend all of our time in admiring ourselves. Rather, loving self means that we do not forget that God has created us and that God has redeemed us. He has also called us to Himself and to His family. If He loves us and has forgiven us, why will we not forgive ourselves?

Some of us cannot forgive ourselves because we have such a low opinion of God's grace toward us especially when we sin. We continue to misunderstand this constant extension of grace by God upon his friends. If we fail to forgive ourselves, then we have said that God's grace and His atonement upon the cross cannot extend to our present sin. That kind of thinking comes from the evil one and goes against the fundamental message of the cross. He has forgiven our sins: past, present and future. If we sin, we confess. When we confess, He forgives. When He forgives, we must forgive ourselves.

As a final note, keep in mind that the prodigal son apparently never regained what he had lost. When it comes to the worst sort of sin where a spouse forgives the other for marital infidelity, God can heal that relationship but only His grace enables the offended one and the offender to cultivate future intimacy. Those who find themselves in such circumstances know the grief and pain of such sin. They also know the time it takes to re-cultivate what sin has destroyed.

> *"As far as the east is from the west so has he removed our transgressions from us."* (Psalm 103.12)

> *"Blessed is the one whose transgression is forgiven, whose sin is covered. Blessed is the man to whom the Lord imputes not iniquity, and in whose spirit there is no guile."* (Psalms 32.1, 2 quote in Romans 4.7, 8)

20

The Added Worth of Change —*Purposely Voluntary.*

"There is no sinless Christian. If you chance upon such a man, he is no Christian but an anti-Christian."

Martin Luther

In a memorable silver screen moment, Forest Gump determines to run literally from the sorrow of an unwanted change in life when his first and only love dies. As his fame grows, eventually everyone wants to run with him across the country. After stepping through the mud on one occasion, a spectator tosses him a towel to clean Gump's face. When Gump returns the towel, the iconic smiley face adorns it. Gump transforms the mud of his sorrow into a symbol for joy and an eventual profit for the bankrupt T-shirt entrepreneur.

Another scene sums up his life of optimism and its effect on others when a running bystander comments to Gump that Forest just ran through a pile of fresh dog droppings. Gump keeps running, shrugs it off and casually says, "It happens."

We may not lead a charmed life like Gump but, like Gump, we cannot avoid change; it happens. Scientists have observed that our expanding universe keeps on racing outward or stretching like a rubber band as some would say. All systems including the human one will wear down eventually and change toward a disintegration. Bolts rust; computers crash; human joints stiffen. Entropy acts unkindly toward everything and everyone. No one and nothing has immunity from change.

Earlier we alluded to Chuck Colson, the hatchet man for Richard Nixon. Even prior to Watergate, those who dealt with this attorney considered him to be a mean if not an evil person. After the Watergate debacle, Americans finally heard about the roughshod manner of this White House advisor. When he put his faith in Christ, those who knew Colson remained unconvinced and skeptical of his conversion. Many former political allies like those in the former White House avoided him. Did they think, "What trick has he devised this time?" Even mature Christians on Capitol Hill failed to accept Colson's conversion. Maybe they could not believe that God could change such a person. If they did think that, then they missed out on what Biblical forgiveness truly means.

Eventually many began to see the validity of his faith by his commitment in the fruit of his conviction. When news reached the general public, it came through the ill-applied idiom by the news outlets, "Colson gets religion." This idiom usually means that someone who has acted badly now acts in a good way because he has made some commitment to God. It also implied that again Colson was marketing a ruse to escape any negative future. What

Colson did and accomplished for Christ pushed him way beyond religionists with their unbending commitment to ritual, rites and traditions. God employed his changed life to change others.

Everyone who knows Jesus Christ has the potential, privilege and power to change. Will the friend of God choose to change?

Does the Gospel bring change now on earth?

The friends of God may inadvertently present their case for becoming a Christian as only an issue of going to Heaven after you die. Such argument could put a relationship to Christ on a par with a rite—a rite of membership by an action of faith at a point in time. Once you have placed your faith in Him, then you have confidence that at death He takes you into His Heaven. They describe that opportunity as being able to have a wonderful life with God after death. No lack of truth comes in that statement. But, it does not present the whole truth.

The Gospel unequivocally answers these two questions:

* *What happens when I die and I know God?*
* *What happens to me now that I know God?*

This chapter deals with the other part of the truth about being God's friend—what happens in this present life before death and an eventual resurrection? Eventual resurrection will mark a dramatic, unforgettable one-time instant transformation for every friend of God. That change will be wonderfully unavoidable and come certainly at the desire and the timing of Almighty God. While the Bible speaks about this glorious opportunity, can even the wildest imagination envision such an event?

As His friends, our life *now* holds as much importance as our life *later*. While later a glorious graduation comes, the immediate now must also be considered. While friends of God may not lead a charmed life like Gump, their change can be positive. God wants to change you not just at resurrection after death but also right now and He offers His friends the privilege to change.

Change takes on all kinds of synonyms: transformation, metamorphosis, growth, spirituality. Theologians give the label of "sanctification" to spiritual change in this earthly life. Although the other synonyms certainly bring insight into this change, sanctification serves as a convenient starting point to speak about change.

Such description can then distinguish it from all other kinds of earthly change. This change does not mean that we focus on doing more but rather that we first focus on being more. As my Fijian friend says, "God made us first as human beings and then called us to be human doings." Change means a maturing in character that affects what we do.

What does sanctification imply?

Sanctification has to do with "sacredness." Sacred implies a quality of dedication or exclusive use. Sacred as a qualifier could extend to a variety of contexts: places, things and writings. Anything that would fit the category of sacred would be considered as "set apart" or "holy." In the Old Testament, the law set apart the priests who served the nation and certain objects that they used in worship as "holy." The change in life to which God calls His friends could be called "holiness" as well as "sanctification."

> *"For God has called us not to impurity but to holiness."* (1 Thessalonians 4.7)

Change for the friend of God implies much but, at the least, it means a setting apart. God expects His friend to set himself apart from the old life that he had. The apostle prays for the church at Ephesus that God would grant them strength "through His Spirit in the inner man." (Ephesians 3.16b) In the language of the New Testament, the word for inner is "*eso.*" It forms the basis for our word "esoteric" which means mysterious, private, or unseen. While aging destroys the "outside" or "exo" part of us, sanctification has to do with the "inside" or "eso" process of positive change. The culture spends much time on the *exo-man* and too little time on the *eso-man.*

The apostle Paul uses both these words in 2 Corinthians 4.16. We know that the outer man or physical body will slowly decay involuntarily in spite of an attempt at fitness and diet. The inner or new man—the spiritual part—of us can continue to grow and to change for the positive. As such, we ought to keep on keeping on in our pursuit of Him that leads to our spiritual maturity.

> *"Therefore, we do not become discouraged although our outer [exo] man is being corrupted yet our inner [eso] man is being renewed day by day."* (Ephesians 3.16)

Change that comes via strength in the "inner" man captures this process of holiness. In the added worth of justification, God has given His friends the standing or position of justification—being declared righteous at a point in time. In the added worth of sanctification, God has asked His friends to take on the process of sanctification—acting right at every point of time in a person's lifetime.

While sanctification grows out of justification and is vitally connected to it, sanctification adds no work to the work that Christ has already accomplished upon the cross in justification. As the friend of God, He will never love you any more or love you any less than He loved you at the moment of His adoption of you as His friend. Change does not have to be a negative like entropy; change can be positive.

How does God expect His friends to be "set apart?"

This setting apart or sanctification works because the Holy Spirit lives within God's friends. Just as the change in status from being God's enemy to being God's friend happens on the basis of God's work on the cross so also does the change from an immature life to a mature life continue on the basis of God's work by His Spirit for enabling in the process of change.

In this process of sanctification, the one who wants to be changed chooses by faith to close the gap between belief in God and behavior for God. Words of faith must begin to match the deeds of faith. This process takes a lifetime and the desire to be wholly changed will only be completed at resurrection.

> *"Being confident of this very thing that He who began a good work in you will complete it in the day of Christ Jesus."* (Philippians 1.6)

Sanctification fuels the deeds of the outer man. James made that clear in his epistle when he argued that genuine faith produces fruit. Just as the issue of friendship with God means more than going to Heaven, a changed life does not begin with obedience to specific commands although it will lead to obedience. Too many times the inner man or inner person is neglected because the deeds of the external receive so much attention. Many stress a list of "do's" and "don'ts" that define a saint's life. Spirituality refuses measurement by attendance at Bible studies, active church involvement or evangelistic endeavors.

From the point of view of God's friend, both justification and sanctification find the mechanism of change in responsibility. In terms of justification, a person had to exercise a one-time genuine and right choice: a decision of faith to experience God as a friend. In terms of sanctification, a person has to exercise many times right choices: decisions of faithfulness to experience a life of sanctification. Faithfulness like faith builds itself upon a biblical foundation. Spirituality means a maturation of character, a habitual change in the "inner" you that produce an "outer" look. It begins with a change within privately before others see a change outwardly. The setting apart process works its way from the inside out. No one can be set apart until that person makes a considered choice. Setting apart a life to serve your Friend will always begin with a consideration about your Friend. As we look at who He is and what He has done for us, that ought to fuel our desire to change and to be like Him.

What under-girds this process of sanctification?

For the one who knows the Lord Jesus Christ, scriptural spirituality implies the ability to know God and to commune with Him because of the presence of His Spirit within each believer. This marks out part of what biblical theology teaches about communion with and worship of God. That person must come in Spirit and in truth. For the Christian that means a commitment to His Word ("Your Word is truth." John 17.17) and to His conviction ("The Spirit shall convict of sin and of righteousness." John 16.8).

Sanctification flows out of an understanding and practice of the Word of God and out of the equipping and patience of other gifted friends of God. We find the words of God in the Bible, His special revelation to us. Just as a person must eat, swallow and digest physical food to live, so also a person must feed on spiritual food in order to grow up into maturity. The writers whom Jesus commissioned delivered to us the exact Word that God desired in the original writings. Today, as respected conservative scholars attest, the friend of God can have absolute confidence that he does have the Word of God that he holds in his hands in his own language.

> *"Each and every Scripture is breathed out by God and profitable for teaching, for reproof, for correction, for discipline and for training in righteousness in order that the man of God may be capable and equipped for every good work."* (2 Timothy 3.16, 17)

> *"For no prophecy [of Scripture] was ever brought forward by an act of the will of man but men who were carried along by the Holy Spirit who spoke from God."* (2 Peter 1.21)

Sanctification also flows out of a relationship of a superior to an inferior. We alluded to this earlier in Chapter Sixteen on the added worth of stewardship. While many of those who actually do know God as a friend attend regularly gatherings of saints on Sunday morning, does that mean that they have the necessary equipping to grow in their holiness? You could liken it to eating just that one big meal at the local restaurant or at the house of the mother-in-law on Sunday after the religious event. Could you survive physically on just that one meal per week?

Equipping also goes by a variety of names: discipleship, mentoring, coaching, or training. Fundamentally, an immature and slightly sanctified person needs the equipping of a more mature person in order to grow up. In the role of discipleship, when a brother or sister continues to sin or to act lawlessly, then a brother or sister must confront that person.

If a person claims to know Christ and has marital infidelity or cheats in business or abuses others, then that person must be confronted. This confrontation—if the person repents and changes his behavior—can lead to growth and to change. This may sound ugly in a society that neglects or dismisses relationships but it remains obligatory in those who follow Christ. We glibly quote, "Faithful are the wounds of a friend," but who wants to put the word-sword into a friend?

The process of discipleship does not turn a disciple into the disciple-maker. The process transforms the disciple into a person who matures and develops a variety of skills. The disciple-maker hopes that his disciple will someday be a disciple-maker himself and grow more mature than the original disciple-maker.

God gave spiritual gifts and ministries to every one of His friends. These gifts and ministries enable the more mature to equip or to train the less mature. This process of accountability in relationships among God's friends contributes to the added worth of change that God has guaranteed. This exercise of gifts and ministries in the lives of others yields great change when the less mature one remains teachable and therefore open to the equipping of the more mature one.

What challenges our sanctification?

My carnal not yet eradicated sin nature permits me to oppose God. Yes, the friend of God now finds that he has a new nature and has a new creation.

> *"Therefore, if anyone is in Christ, he is a new creation; the old things have passed away. The brand new has come."* (2 Corinthians 5.17)

However, as humans, we make choices. In spite of an indwelling Holy Spirit, the friends of God may yet oppose Him. They could oppose Him because of ignorance but the study of His Word cures ignorance. The friend of God may choose not to practice what he has discovered in His Word. Our disobedience could oppose Him.

I ought to choose God in my growth but I may choose myself and my desires. I may choose a moral life which has merit. I may choose a materially profitable life which has merit. I may choose a service life which has merit. But, nothing has merit if it has its source beyond His desires. The most important questions are: "How do you know when you are in the flesh?" "How do you know when you act carnally?"

Sanctification also means an ongoing struggle in an internal fight. A popular bumper sticker states, "Christians are not perfect just forgiven." The absolute perfection that eliminates internal strife ends only at the graduation into eventual glorification. Until then, the friend of God will fail self, fail others and, simply put, will just not do every time what God wants him to do. The added worth of change means that the friend of God measures a success of faithfulness over a lifetime and not just in the moments of failure. And what God wants always benefits His friend. The battle within may not be won every day; but, over a lifetime, the change from serving self to serving God and others comes as a great added benefit to living out this life.

As part of change, the friend of God can manifest the presence of God by demonstrating change among earth-dwellers by having inward godly motives and outward godly actions. When God's friends do good works for Him and explain it as such, He receives the honor because then they glorify Him. In that sense, the saint now shares the glory of God. How do you measure such an added worth as that?

We ought not to separate the earthly from the Heavenly just as we ought not to separate the secular from the spiritual. Graduation has to do with ultimate glory in eternity. Sanctification has to do with present glory on earth. Graduation has to do with product or purpose; sanctification has to do with the concept of process. Change must work its way from the inside out as the progress of change reveals a performance of change. But, the performance must absolutely be linked to and sourced in the inward choice to change.

Change does not just randomly happen as Gump has suggested. Change means choice.

What's so great about change?

Change in God's sense of change means that you get to grow up. You gain confidence by experiencing both the cost and benefit of change. You begin to live smartly as you cultivate the rightful role of a wise liver. You relish the opportunity to see life from a perspective beyond yourself because your subjective and small perspective cannot really give the needful interpretation for life that God brings. Finally, you know that having a steadfast, unmovable work for Him cannot be anything less than eventually rewarding because you have learned of the mercy of your Friend.

Gaining the added worth of change by God comes as part of trusting Jesus Christ, His Son. The indwelling Spirit and the indwelling Word remain indispensable to true spirituality. The one who lives in the household of God cannot forget either.

> *"I am confident of this very thing that He who began a good work in you will complete it in the day of Christ Jesus."* (Philippians 1.6)

Every person on earth lives here by His permission. We can only graduate into glory because He has put the glory of the gospel into our hearts. In spite of others' denials, only His granted privilege keeps us here to work, to love and to live.

So, why do I act so independently? Why do I act as if I am the source, cause or ground of existence? A Christian who chooses to act in such a way runs the risk of divine discipline for such anti-Biblical or sub-Christian thinking.

God has granted you the privilege to know Him. He has not necessarily granted you the privilege to escape your earthly problems. Your problems act as a mirror to reveal your need to depend upon Him. He could grant you relief or He could permit you to suffer under His kind hand of discipline.

On the outside, sanctification or growth is reflected in godly behavior. On the inside, sanctification or growth is rooted in godly dependence. While a person may demonstrate godly behavior on the outside, the true Christian will struggle against the flesh on the inside.

We must ask: "Does it bring glory to God?" "Does it honor Him?"

> *"Whether you eat or drink or whatsoever you do, do all for the glory of God."* (1 Corinthians 10.31)

21

The Added Worth of Suffering —*an Involuntary Change*

"God whispers to us in our pleasures, speaks in our conscience, but shouts in our pains; it is His megaphone to rouse a deaf world."

C. S. Lewis

"Indeed, I can say with complete truthfulness that everything I have learned in my seventy-five years in this world, everything that has truly enhanced and enlightened my existence, has been through affliction and not through happiness, whether pursued or attained."

Malcolm Muggeridge,
journalist and former outspoken agnostic

Not every child gets to spend time with his father. In my case, my father spent enough time with me. My father had a day job but his passion lay in growing vegetables and in carpentry. On this particular day, the call of my playmates had a stronger pull than being the shadow of my father. As my father cleaned his brushes in the cellar of our home, an explosion ignited the small room. My father ran out of the cellar, grabbed my mother's throw rugs and put out the fire that could have destroyed the house. In the process, he sustained serious burns on his legs and arms. His recovery went slowly and painfully especially in the 1950's of America. But, what a relative said about his predicament delivered a different kind of pain.

While he remained in the hospital, this well-meaning relative who claimed to know Christ came to his room and explained to him the cause of his suffering. To reconstruct others' recollection, she spoke in this way, "You are here because God is punishing you. You are in this hospital room and in pain because you have sinned against God."

How much can we say for sure about suffering?

We humans exercise a sometimes troublesome but natural trait. We want to be able to know and to explain everything. That extends to an explanation to others of the cause of their suffering. One of my mentors said it best: "What God reveals is our business; what is not revealed is not our business." In this context in terms of people's plight about suffering, we know with certainty that what God has revealed comes from His Word. All other explanations about life's evils and problems tend toward speculation.

What has God revealed about suffering? Scripture argues that suffering comes from five sources:

1. World
2. Others

3. Satan
4. God
5. Myself

Whatever may be the source of our suffering, suffering highlights our weakness and our finiteness. Suffering forces us to move from our list of trivial needs to what we really need. Suffering can put us on our knees, cause us to fall down in worship or make us raise our closed fist in anger toward God or others. My playmates unknowingly kept me from suffering that day. But, my father used the observations of a relative as an excuse to keep himself away from God for a very long time.

The world and others can bring us suffering.

The world has its hazards. Anyone who has been backpacking in the wilderness accepts the dangers that come with being in the outdoors. You could face a bear or a mountain lion or even awesome terrain that could bring disaster. The world in terms of nature can also cause suffering. Recent years in America have listed many lost lives in major snowstorms, hurricanes and tornadoes. Around the world, awful weather that includes tsunamis has brought death to many and brought millions of dollars of damage. In the world of pleasure, your favorite amusement ride could crash with you in it.

Others can bring us suffering in terms of their selfish pursuits or in terms of their unselfish pursuits. A person on the way to work hurriedly fails to slow down and passes a bus that stops to pick up children. His passing puts the children in danger. Those who drink and drive put the rest of us on the road in danger if they fail to control their vehicle. On the other hand, a surgeon who wants to save lives might inadvertently leave a sponge or some other foreign object in a patient.

Others can cause us to suffer because they know what we believe. In terms of the media, the friend of God may not suffer but his world-view receives snarky, belittling and sometimes downright unfounded criticism. Those in fairly public arenas find themselves and their faith the target of ridicule. This certainly causes us sorrow but we ought to expect that from the world.

In terms of physical suffering, every apostle except John died as a result of suffering for their faith. Today, in many countries, the friends of God suffer and sometimes give their lives for their faith. These places would include Libya, China, Sudan, Nigeria, Kenya, Egypt, India, Vietnam, Burma and Malaysia just to mention a few. Peter considers such suffering as a blessing.

> *"If you are insulted for the name of Christ, you are blessed because the Spirit and glory of God rests upon you."* (1 Peter 5.14)

Life has its risk of suffering. It comes as part of living in a fallen world among fallen people. Jesus warned his disciples that they could expect suffering if they would follow Him.

> *"These things I have spoken to you so that in me you may have peace. In the world you will have affliction*

but take courage. I have victory over the world." (John 16.33)

In a way that the world cannot understand, God uses the affliction that others deliver to gain our attention. If we respond by praising God then we can speak as Alexander Solzhenitsyn did after the Soviets released this so-called dissident.

"I bless you prison—I bless you for being in my life —for there lying on rotting prison straw, I learned the object of life is not prosperity as I had grown up believing, but the maturing of the soul."

Our stewardship as His ambassador can bring suffering. The apostle Paul speaks of this ambassadorship as one of weakness and of suffering. He alluded to the suffering that he faced by just traveling in the Roman world and to the suffering that he faced in representing the Gospel. In spite of this suffering, he saw it as light affliction in terms of an eventual glorious reward.

"For our momentary light affliction is producing for us a more exceeding weight of glory." (2 Corinthians 4.17)

Satan can bring us suffering

The late comedian Flip Wilson used to dress as a woman as the character Geraldine and proclaim the following excuse as the reason for her promiscuity: "The devil made me do it." He got a lot of laughs for that phrase and many people would regularly use that quote in conversation for any shortcoming or offense toward others. But, we cannot joke about a being so dangerous and so evil. Satan does exist and he is mentioned in every book of the New Testament.

As the once beautiful being among the rest of the angels, he sought in his pride the awful position of ascending above God and usurping God's authority. (Isaiah 1.13-14) While God has rendered a verdict of guilty (John 12.31) and a punishment of eventual condemnation, Satan still patrols the earth. He acts as the god of this age (2 Corinthians 4.4) and rules as the prince of the power of the air (Ephesians 3.2) as the ruler of this fallen world.

In spite of Satan's power, God limits it. The book of Job illustrates this point best. Satan can only do what God permits. As the book opens, Satan enters the presence of God along with the angels and challenges God to present someone on earth who manifests uprightness. God answers, "Have you not considered my servant Job because there is none like him on the earth, a perfect and upright man who fears God and turns away from evil?" (Job 1.8)

God permits Satan to test Job without killing him to prove to Satan that men can continue to worship and to serve God just as God and not for what God gives man. The book also contributes to understanding our relationship as the friend of God. Those whom He has declared righteous continue to worship and to remain loyal to God in spite of tremendous suffering.

Satan operates in various venues along with his fallen angels. Overall, he wants to stop the work of God by blinding the minds of the lost (2 Corinthians 4.4), by deceiving the nations (Revelation 20.3) and tempting the saints to immorality (1 Corinthians 7.5). The apostles Paul and Peter warn the friends of God to understand the conflict that we face, be on guard for Satan and put on our armor through prayer. This ought not to give us fear since our friend, the Lord Jesus, has defeated the evil one and only what He permits may enter into our lives for His glory and thus for our benefit.

> *"... the struggle for us is not against blood and flesh but against the rulers, against the authorities, against the cosmic powers of this darkness, against the evil spiritual forces in the heavenly places."* (Ephesians 6.12)

> *"Be sober minded, be alert because your enemy the devil as a roaring lion is prowling about and seeking someone to devour."* (1 Peter 5.8)

God can permit suffering for our sake.

Knowing God does not give us a pass from suffering. Job comes to mind as the most obvious example. Job had done nothing yet God permitted Satan to use Job as evidence to Satan and now to us that those who know God must worship Him no matter the cost. This cost comes out quite clearly when disciples wanted to continue to follow Jesus. He made it clear that the one whom they wanted to follow had no place to lay His head and neither would they. They might also have to leave their family. (See Luke 9.57-62)

The ancient world assumed symmetry in suffering. Hindus pretty much still believe that today. This frightening concept says that every time that you suffer you must have done something wrong. In the case of the blind man (John 9), even the disciples considered the answer to the blind man as a result of his sin or his parents' sin. Jesus made it clear that the healing of the man's blindness would manifest the work of God for His glory.

The same holds true for Mary and Martha. Jesus knew that they were grieving because He later wept when He met them on the way to their house. Although He knew that the sisters would have joy in the resurrection of their brother, he knew that Lazarus had died and that He would raise him. Yet, He also had tremendous sorrow as the sisters did and demonstrated it with His weeping. In spite of His and their grief, He waited until Lazarus had definitely died so that His resurrection would manifest His glory and prove that He had the credentials to be the Messiah of Israel and the Savior of the world. In the case of the apostle Paul, God gave him "a thorn in the flesh, a messenger of Satan to buffet" him. (2 Corinthians 12.7)

Bad things just do not happen to "bad" people but to all people. Somehow we think that, if we are good, then we ought not to suffer. This kind of cause and effect thinking not only makes things worst, it goes against the way life really is. We then try to control the suffering by reliving the past and rethinking how the suffering could have been avoided. To a certain degree that makes sense if the examination focuses upon bad habits or bad company that needs to be changed.

The friend of God can cause his own suffering.

"A sanctified person [is] like a silver bell, the harder he is smitten the better he soundeth."

George Swinnock, Puritan writer

I cannot forget my Little League season circa 1958 not because I batted .000 but because one of the star players drowned in the Ohio River. The team went to the funeral and formed a cordon for the pallbearers as someone else raised in salute the bat that I had brought. All of us used to take chances by swimming in creeks, ponds and abandoned quarries. We also jumped from bridges and overhanging trees with or without ropes oblivious to hidden objects in the water below as we mimicked Johnny Weissmuller.

Very few though ever swam in the powerful pull of the Ohio. Certainly people fished or skied on the river but few chose to swim. When the local bridge collapsed one Christmas, some plant workers chose not to drive the extra miles to another bridge to go to work on the West Virginia side. One group decided to take regularly a boat directly across each day and evening and save the distance. One winter, the father of a teenager friend died when the workers' boat capsized.

We make no judgment here as to all the decisions that went into the reasons that led to the deaths that we mentioned. Certainly the coroner listed accidental as the causes of death. Others might label such deaths with the legal phrase "an act of God." Insurers label any loss of life or property as acts of God when no foresight could have prevented the accident. In such cases they will not pay or do not want to pay for loss of property. This could include earthquakes, tornadoes, unforeseen high tides and maybe even overturned boats on wintry rivers. Nonetheless, choices have consequences.

We all have the capacity to make choices that can bring suffering and even death. Even those who call themselves the friends of God can find themselves tempted and succumb to choices that lead to sin that brings suffering. We can even make choices that cause God to bring some sort of discipline to return us to Him. The writer to the Hebrews argues that the discipline of God which could include suffering benefits the recipient.

> *"All discipline does not seem joyful for the moment but painful. Nevertheless, afterwards, it produces the peaceable fruit of righteousness to those who have been trained by it."*(Hebrews 12.11)

Saints cannot treat His discipline lightly because He disciplines us with love as a cause and with growth in mind as a benefit. Jesus received the punishment of God the Father not because He sinned but because we had. He persevered all the way to the point of shedding blood and giving up His life. He has called us to such perseverance although our suffering and death has nothing to do at all with paying for our sins. The writer to the Hebrews made this observation on the benefits of the discipline of God as the Father.

Discipline by the Father in Heaven benefits His friends in these ways:

1. It proves God's love for us. (12.6) Disobedience to His Word thwarts growth and hinders our relationship to Him. His imposition of unpleasant consequences may move the saint back to a life of obeying and honoring Him.
2. It proves sonship in the family of God.(12.7) It used to be that the unconditional love and consistent discipline of a parent proved the children's legitimacy in that family. Discipline would manifest itself in appropriate punishment and regular training. Only illegitimate children had no opportunity for this proof.
3. It makes the sons respect the fathers. (12.9) People find this difficult to accept. If the argument holds true that discipline does indeed have a positive effect, then the respect comes because the son understands that the father is willing to make the son suffer even if briefly and slightly so that he can grow.
4. It enables the sons to share in holiness. (12.10) God regenerates every saint and thereby makes each one a sharer of his holiness in that he has a new nature that he never had before (2 Corinthians 5.17) and he has the indwelling of the Spirit. (Ephesians 1.13) Yet, as the New Testament writ-

ers argue, we may quench the Spirit. (1 Thessalonians 5.19) So, we must be diligent in our pursuit of godliness. (2 Peter 1.5)

5. It produces the fruit of righteousness. (12.11) John the apostle speaks of God as the vinedresser in John 15 where God raises up or prunes the branches so that they may bear more fruit.

"God has twisted together His glory and our good."
Thomas Watson, Puritan, (1620-1686)

How should we respond to suffering?

"I do not know the answer to the problem of evil, but I do know love."
Alyosha speaks in the Brothers Karamazov

The classic fairy tale ends with these well-known words, "And they lived happily ever after." They could live happily ever after because wrongs were righted, the evil ones received punishment or banishment and the main characters who suffered now have wonderful lives. The genre of the fairy tale finds its basis in what God has declared about our final destination. His friends will rule in some way as His heirs. In the meantime, how ought we to live with suffering?

First, let's be careful about declaring the cause of my own or anyone else's suffering. Since suffering comes from a variety of sources, can we truly identify the source of others' suffering? Worst yet, would we want to be the ones who decide why others suffer? In our individual case, however, we would be wise to examine our lives to see if sin has caused us to suffer.

Next, we must be careful about unrealistic expectations or incomplete understanding. This comes especially in the area of culture and politics. We think that our view ought to dominate the whole of the culture. Yet, we know that God brings about political circumstances and resultant suffering because of His interests. He used Nebuchadnezzar and the pagan Babylonians to discipline Israel and, in turn, suffering to his prophet Jeremiah who had preached for some forty years for those in Jerusalem and in Judah to repent. Too many times we think that we suffer because the culture has abandoned our values or our guy has failed to get elected or justice has fled.

What we consider unpleasant God may consider necessary. When the brothers of Joseph sold him to the Ishmaelites, Joseph suffered even more in Egypt by being wrongly accused. Even when he ascended to be a co-ruler of the nation, he suffered in missing his family. However, God used him as a tool to bless the world by saving his family and the whole nation of Israel. We cannot know the whole story on our suffering but we do know the One who knows us and knows of our suffering. As Martin Luther stated,

"We will commit sins while we are here, for this life is not a place where justice resides. We, however, says Peter (2 Peter 3:13), are looking forward to a new heaven and a new earth where justice will reign."

Third, suffering no matter the source or the cause gives the friend of God the opportunity to grow and to bear more fruit for Him. No one naturally wants to suffer but adversity develops our character.

> "... *we boast in our tribulations because we know that tribulation works out endurance and endurance approval and approval hope and hope does not disappoint because the love of God has been poured out in our hearts through the Holy Spirit who was given to us.*" (Romans 4.3-5)

Rough trials and deep grief in our journey through life cultivates our maturity as the saint learns to depend upon God. Tribulations and trials exercise our spiritual muscles. Saints ought to change in character as a prime expectation of the life in Christ. Suffering comes as part of the mysteries that we endure because we cannot see the whole picture or the end of life as God has purposed it. May we agree with Paul the apostle in understanding about our holiness:

> "*I am well-pleased with weaknesses, with insults, with distresses, with persecutions and with difficulties for the sake of Christ because when I am weak He is strong.*" (2 Corinthians 12.10)

Fourthly, He does not leave us alone in our suffering and comes to comfort us in our suffering. We choose to continue to wonder "Why?" and stay stuck on ourselves in a selfish and unproductive way. Or, we choose to work with the "Who?" in that we look to Him and see our comfort in Him.

> *"Come to me all you who are wearied and burdened. I will give you rest. Take up my yoke and learn from me because I am gentle and humble in heart and find rest for your souls because my yoke is easy to bear and my burden is light."* (Matthew 11.28-30)

Finally, suffering does not keep us from having joy in our lives now. No one will ever suffer as Jesus suffered. Only He could suffer to the point of shedding blood so that we may live. In spite of His sufferings, He endured them because He knew that at the end glory awaited Him as He honored the Father who had sent Him. Jesus endured the suffering and shame and considered it joy because, at the end, He would sit at the right hand of the Father and be returned to the glory that He once had. (Hebrews 12.1-3)

Paul the apostle considered his time in prison as worthwhile. He had visited Rome on his second missionary journey as recorded in Acts 16. He wrote to the Philippians from prison and in that short epistle of some 2000 or so words in English, he uses the word "rejoice" nine times and "joy" five times. From the suffering of prison, he considered the joy as beneficial to him because it brought glory to God through the conversion of the lost that would be guarding him or through the growth of the saints who heard about his suffering and used him as encouragement in their suffering.

"Christ's work, both in the church and in the hearts of Christians, often goes backward so that it may go forward better. As seed rots in the ground in the winter time, but after comes up better and the harder the winter the more flourishing the spring, so we learn to stand by falls, and get strength by weakness discovered. We take deeper root by shaking."

Richard Sibbes, Puritan, The Bruised Reed

Television network shows resolve problems in twenty-two minutes or fifty-two minutes except maybe the soap operas that go on for many seasons and many years. But, suffering may last a life time for a Christian. Suffering has its place in our life. Even the discipline from God may not seem joyful but at the end the process of discipline produces the product of ultimate joy. We can endure suffering from any source because we know that our ultimate final destination will bring us such joy.

We don't survive and grow in suffering by knowledge but by abiding in the love that God through the Lord Jesus has for His friends.

> *"Therefore, since we have so great a cloud of witnesses, let us lay aside every impediment and the sin that surrounds us and let us run with endurance the race that is before us as we fix our eyes on Jesus, the pioneer and perfecter of our faith who for the joy ahead of Him endured the cross as he despised the shame and sat down at the right hand of the Father."* (Hebrews 12.1-3)

22

The Added Worth of Graduation —*a Guaranteed Ultimate Change*

"At the end of the game, the king and the pawn go back in the same box."

An Italian proverb

"A funeral is one day when everyone remembers you and then forgets you forever."

Mark Twain

On that cold November day those who stood with the bereaved manifested more practical wisdom than I. The men and women all wore heavy, dark overcoats. In spite of my lack of practical wisdom, I had come to share true wisdom of the gospel. Love had motivated these men and women to come and show their sympathy for the survivors by attending this gravesite ceremony of the loved one who had passed beyond this present earth. On that day, they heard words like these, "No one wants to come to a cemetery and, on this day, you made a decision to come. On the other hand, someday someone will carry you to a place like this. If you know that you will someday come involuntarily, will you now voluntarily think about what that means and what you can do about it?"

Misinformation fills our culture and thus our minds in what happens after death. The bereaved father may say this about the premature death of his daughter, "She is now the prettiest angel in Heaven." The wife of my childhood minister told the story of the little boy who died, went to Heaven and had a place of honor as an angel because he acted so humbly. Others talk about wings, harps and seats on clouds.

As a whole the American culture has a curiosity sometimes bizarre and not verified about life after death. The secular as well as the religious world has published books about life after death experiences. Many rank as best sellers maybe because they all tend to relate positive experiences.

The friend of God cannot rely upon others' experiences. He must rely upon the Word to discover what it means to graduate from this earth and these earthly bodies and into glory. We must also discover what happens to the friends of God after they die because our ultimate end determines our present desires and practices. How can we do now unless we know now of our destination later?

What did the disciples experience at the transfiguration of Jesus?

One day in the last year of His ministry Jesus promised three of His disciples that they would not taste death before they saw the kingdom of God come with power. Since Jesus ascended into the heavens and did not establish His kingdom then on earth, when did they see it? They saw it around one week later after He made the promise. This happened when Jesus ascended with Peter, James and John up a high mountain. [Scholars would choose Mt. Carmel or Mt. Hermon.]

Theologians call this moment the Transfiguration. Three gospel accounts record it: Matthew 17.1-9, Luke 9.27-36, and Mark 9.2-10. In this event, both Moses and Elijah appeared and talked with Jesus about His departure from the earth as the disciples act as spectators in the gallery. We want to make some observations about this singular moment in the life of Christ that contributes to our understanding of the graduation of the friend of God.

On that mountain Jesus underwent a temporary metamorphosis. What glory that His human body had shielded now burst forth for a moment in glory as bright as the sun so that his garments appeared in brilliant white. Luke describes his face and clothes as white as lightning. In the Old Testament as Moses spoke with God, his face began to shine with the glory of God. That glory eventually faded. In the case of Jesus, the glory came from within, radiated out and temporarily liberated itself from the human body that constrained it.

Jesus conversed with both Moses and Elijah. Interpreters have debated why these two appeared to Jesus. Certainly their abilities to do signs and wonders marked them as two with important divine authority. Somehow at some point the gospel writers understood and identified the two as Moses and Elijah. Moses never entered the Promised Land because after God spoke to him on the mountain, he died without any suffering. God Himself then buried

Moses in a spot where no man knew. (Deuteronomy 34.5, 6) On the other hand, Elijah never died. After he concluded his ministry and among his school of disciples, he ascended into the sky in a whirlwind as chariots and horses of fire accompanied him. (1 Kings 2.1-11)

How does the transfiguration of Jesus help us understand graduation?

Graduation into eventual glory does not change the identity of a person. In other words, humans do not turn into angels or animals or any other sort of earthly creature. We do not know how the disciples identified Moses and Elijah nor do we know the bodies that they had. But, after graduation—death of Moses, the living ascension of Elijah—Moses remained as Moses and Elijah continued to be Elijah. After their entrance into glory, they yet had an existence that included the knowledge of the eventual return of Jesus to glory.

All people who die have an eternal existence in spite of what many religions teach about life after death. Those who do not know God will also exist after death but with punishment as the enemies of God deserve. They will not be annihilated nor will they be re-cycled back on earth in someone else's earthly body. Scripture argues throughout its extent that humans do not quit existing once they have been created in the womb no matter the time of their demise.

Graduation from this body and into His presence means a consciousness. Many might argue that at death you enter a state of unconscious sleep like state. In this case at the transfiguration, both Moses and Elijah acted in a wide awake manner. The apostle Paul argues further for this idea when he said, "I am pressed between the two: having a desire to depart and be with Jesus for that is far better but it is necessary to remain with you all." (Philippians 1.23, 24) Whether the apostle lived or died, he saw it as gain. For him, this life just continued on into another life after graduation that liberated him from this old and corrupted body. He saw graduation from here as an immediate presence with Jesus.

What does graduation mean for the friends of God?

What we do here now has an effect on our welcoming party later. The parable of the unrighteous steward supports this idea. (Luke 16.1-9) When the unrighteous steward knew that he had lost his employment, he contacted all the debtors of his master. The steward gained the debtors' loyalty and friendship by reducing considerably their debt to the master. When the master found this out, he commended the unrighteous steward for his shrewdness not his dishonesty.

Jesus comments on this when He says, "Make friends for yourselves by means of the mammon of unrighteousness so that when it fails they may receive you into everlasting dwellings." (Luke 16.9) What we do cannot possibly ever be the first cause of the salvation of another but God honors our ancillary or secondary contributions. The support of ourselves and others as we give our wealth to the work of the proclamation of the Gospel contributes to the continuance of the gospel worldwide.

What we do here now has an effect on our rewards later. We have alluded to this earlier in our section on stewardships. The apostle Paul wrote about this in his letters to the congregation at Corinth. (1 Corinthians 3.10-15, 2 Corinthians 5.10) After the friend of God graduates, he will eventually face a judgment but not for salvation. That happened at the cross. The judgment seat has the name of *Bema*. In literature this seat has the idea of reward associated with it. At this seat, the friend of God faces an evaluation for his performance. This judgment does not look at sin but at the worth in terms of faithfulness of what we do. You may suffer loss because you built unwisely but you will still be saved. Eternal life is forever. Once it begins it cannot stop. If it did, it would not be eternal life.

What we do here now has no effect on some things that we will receive later. Now, this may sound contradictory to the previous statement. This statement concerns what the Heavenly Father gives to every friend of His no matter the level of his performance.

He has reserved an inheritance for us.

> *"Praise be the God and Father of our Lord Jesus Christ who according to his great mercy has given us a new birth to a living hope through the resurrection of Jesus Christ from the dead, and into an inheritance imperishable, undefiled, unfaded and protected in heaven for you."* (1 Peter 1.3, 4)

He has given us immediate entry into His presence at graduation.

"We are confident, I say, and would prefer to be away from the body and at home with the Lord. So we make it our goal to please Him, whether we are at home in the body or away from it." (2 Corinthians 5.8, 9)

He motivates us because of His guaranteed inheritance.

"Whatever you do, work at it with all your heart, as for the Lord, not for men since you know that you will receive an inheritance from the Lord as a reward. It is the Lord Christ you are serving." (Colossians 3.23-24)

He has guaranteed us the hope of glorification.

"Beloved, now we are the children of God and not yet has it been made known what we will be. We know that when he appears, we shall be like him, for we shall see him as he is. Everyone who has this hope in him purifies himself, just as he is pure." (1 John 3.2-3)

"When Christ who is your life shall appear, you will appear with Him in glory." (Colossians 3.4)

He has granted us a Heavenly citizenship.

"But our citizenship is in heaven. And we eagerly await a Savior from there—the Lord Jesus Christ—who will transform our humble body so that they will be like his glorious body by the work of His power to subject all things to Himself." (Philippians 3.20, 21)

What does graduation mean for the friend of God?

One monument dominates a cemetery in Bridgeport, Connecticut. The designer of that monument whose body rests beneath it also secretly built a larger than life statue of himself to be erected in the city park after his death. Nearby an indistinguishable stone used to mark out another's demise until her friends erected a somewhat larger stone some fifty years after her death.

Sometimes, how much people leave in granite and marble reveals what they think about themselves. The larger monument belongs to "America's greatest entertainer," one of the first of America's millionaires and a hoaxer who appealed to people's more prurient interests—P. T. Barnum. The smaller marker belongs to Fanny Crosby, the blind and prolific writer who gave American Christendom its greatest hymns. Fanny, in spite of her friends' later actions, made it clear that as little as possible should mark her grave. She wanted money spent on living people and not a dead monument of marble.

No one likes to think about cemeteries. But, cemeteries keep man from denying his destination. Man does get old, decays and dies. Whole industries have arisen to fulfill the demands of a rapidly expanding market of people who want to slow down the process of aging, to cope with the anxieties of aging or to mask the effects of aging. While topical procedures may temporarily banish life's wrinkles or transform the crown of our heads, we cannot stop the ongoing march of personal entropy. We all want to avoid this negative change but we cannot. Bodies wear out and are laid down usually quite involuntarily and put away deep enough where others cannot see the awful ruin.

Mark Twain did not know God so he failed to know that one person never forgets you. The friend of God who dies has immediately graduated into the presence of the Lord. Only later do friends and family conduct the funeral as the ceremony of the graduation. Upon that person has been conferred the eligibility to go on to a different degree of living. As to the Italian proverb, all persons will die but we do not all have the same destination. The enemy of God receives his inglorious degree of condemnation; the friend of God receives the glorious degree of commendation and eventual glorification.

What now ought we to do in light of graduation?

God has called us to go to a country that we have not seen but where we belong. Until He calls us there, we act in accordance with that destination. Americans speak of retirement; but, in terms of Christian responsibility, retirement comes at the grave. Until then, we act as if we know the place where we go next because we know the one

Pioneer and Perfecter of our faith who has gone ahead to prepare a place for us.

A glorified object radiates splendor and reserves honor for the source of glory. While God's friends wait for being with Him in His presence to experience such splendor, God's perspective differs. He looks at the tape of the finish line and considers His friends as already glorified. He guarantees that all His friends will partake in glory.

What kind of private celebration beyond this temporal reality awaits the friend of God? Immediately at death, the friend of God will find himself in the presence of the Lord Himself. The friend of God will have escaped the pain that this life of decay brings. The friend of God will no longer have to fight within to choose to serve God and not to serve self. The friend of God will finally see face-to-face the one who has brought all of this added worth to His creatures. The friend of God will fully realize the Heavenly citizenship. He will at last see those who have gone ahead of Him into His presence.

Gaining the added worth of graduation unto glorification from God comes as part of trusting Jesus Christ, His Son.

> *"Therefore, since we are surrounded by so great a cloud of witnesses, we must throw off every encumbrance and the sin that so easily surrounds us and in diligence run the race that is before us as we fix our eyes upon Jesus, the Pioneer and Perfecter of our faith."* (Hebrews 12.1, 2a)

"In a moment, in the blinking of an eye, at the last trumpet, for the trumpet will sound and the dead shall be raised imperishable and we shall be changed." (1 Corinthians 15 .52)

Reprise

Your Worth Works

"Remember your Creator in the days of your youth, while the days of trouble do not come, nor the years draw near when you shall say, 'I have no pleasure in them.'"

(Ecclesiastes 12.1)

When the apostle Peter ascended on that mountain with Jesus and James and John at the transfiguration, he witnessed what truly deserves the word "awesome." He saw the appearance of two Old Testament saints. He saw the glory of the Lord Himself even if ever so briefly. Peter would not again have such an experience until Jesus returns with all of His friends to judge the world.

Peter had walked up a literal mountain; others confirmed his experience by being there with him; and he came down from that mountain willingly and fully aware of his faculties. He had also heard the Father say as He had said to John the Baptist at the baptism of Jesus, "this is my beloved Son in whom I am well pleased." Peter had seen the grandeur; Peter had heard the voice of God. James and John also saw and they also heard.

How do we know that we know?

> *"For we did not follow cleverly imagined myths when we made known to you the power and coming back of our Lord Jesus Christ. Now, we have been eyewitnesses of his majesty. For He received from God the Father honor and glory, such a voice being uttered to him by the majestic glory: 'This is my beloved Son, in whom I am well pleased'; and this voice we heard spoken from heaven, as we were with him on the holy mountain. So we have the prophetic word made surer, to which you do well to take heed (as to a lamp shining in a dark place) until the day dawns and the morning star arises in your hearts; Know this first of all, that no prophecy of scripture is a matter of one's own imagination for prophecy was not ever uttered by the will of man, but by holy men of God who were carried along by the power of the Holy Spirit."* (2 Peter 1.16-21)

In spite of the certainty of that experience, Peter saw Scripture—the Word of God—as more certain than that. And He had no doubt about his experience upon the mountain when Jesus revealed his majesty.

Peter had truly experienced an unforgettable, once in the history of mankind event; yet, in spite of his absolute certainty of that event, he proclaimed that the Word of God had more reliability than that event. He used the New Testament Greek word *bébaios* underlined above in the passage to describe the reliability of Scripture. The word has a field of meaning that would include fixed, firm, or certain.

Scholars have taken a variety of ways to translate this word. The International Standard Version New Testament describes the Scripture as "confirmed beyond doubt." (2 Peter 1.19) Other translations use the words: "more sure" (NASB, KJV); "altogether reliable" (NET Bible); "more fully confirmed" (ESV); "completely reliable" (NIV) and "more surer" (Darby).

In short, we have an absolutely reliable trustworthy message from God in our Old and New Testaments. From these words, the special revelation of God, we must build our lives. The preceding and lengthy pages have been gleaned honestly from Scripture. No apology must be made for God's words. As to my words, they certainly may contain grammatical or spelling errors but overall an honest and straightforward attempt has been made to explain to you the Christian world-view: what it means to know Jesus and to follow Him.

What should we do with all our worth?

No greater worth can one possess than having God as a friend. Jesus suffered beyond imagination to offer Himself as a sacrifice for sins. Now, He wants His friends to work out by behavior in their lives what they have believed as the Word reveals it. He wants us to choose to prove our friendship to Him as Scripture has said: in obedience and in the power of His indwelling Spirit.

The friend of God has tremendous God-given ability to serve Him. We will never have enough time on this earth to fulfill the potential that He has given us. But, we could start to begin on the inside as we quietly study His Word. His worth works to benefit us and to motivate us.

"Most of man's troubles come from his not being able to sit quietly in his chamber."

Blaise Pascal

Have you neglected your worth for other pursuits?

When the people rejected Jesus in Galilee, He began to speak in parables or extended analogies that usually came in story form. These parables obscured the truth for those outside of the school of disciples, for those who chose not to believe in Jesus. In private, Jesus would explain the meaning of the parable to the twelve. We mentioned earlier the most famous parable that spoke of the prodigal son. (Luke

15.11-31) The title "Seeking Father" might fit the parable better because the two previous parables (Luke 15.3-10) have to do with seeking a lost sheep and seeking a lost coin.

Most of us know about the two sons. We have spent most of our time on the wasteful or prodigal son. As the younger son, he demanded his inheritance, departed from the country of the father, squandered his possessions in a far country and then returned to be accepted by His Father.

Jesus gave this parable to answer the question, "Does God care about sinners?" Jesus proved that God cared by spending time with sinners and, of course, dying on the cross for sinners. As a friend of God, even on a daily basis, you may be down that highway away from the Father's house. But, He has never left you and He wants you to return, reckon yourself dead to sin and continue that race to follow Him. Where do you find yourself?

Are you in the far country, away from the Father and in wasteful pursuits?

Are you in the near country where the Father lives and in rewarding pursuits?

Are you in between: going away to the far country or returning to the near country?

This parable goes on to say that even the angels in Heaven rejoice when a sinner repents. In that case, it refers directly to those who still sit as God's enemies and outside of Christ. We could safely assume that angels who wonder about our nature and our actions and rejoice when we repent could also rejoice when we return from the far country that each of us has created when we drift away from God, the Father. (1 Peter 1.12)

"Likewise, I say unto you, there is joy in the presence of the angels of God over one sinner who repents." (Luke 15.10)

Worth Returning

The last written book of the canon, the book of the *Revelation of Jesus Christ* challenges us as to its interpretation. A joke goes like this. Some young and immature seminarians regularly played basketball at this public gym. One day they saw an elderly man who handed out the towels and was reading the Bible. One seminarian asked, "Sir, what are you reading?" He replied, "Revelation." The smart aleck student who had studied the book said, "Do you know what it means?" The elderly gentlemen responded quickly, "I do not know all that it means, young man, except this one idea, 'Jesus wins!'"

The early church regularly anticipated the return of Jesus. Sometimes they quit working because they thought he was coming. The apostle Paul corrected that thinking when he wrote to the church at Thessalonica. He reminded them to work and to wait. Of course, the biblical idea of waiting means anticipating.

Our final and full sense of His worth will be realized when He returns to judge and to rule and we experience a new body, a new heaven and a new earth. Until then, may we work out the worth that He has loaned us, do the business that he has given us and wait eagerly for His return.

Ultimate Hope of Worth

"And then I saw a new Heaven and a new earth for the first Heaven and the first earth had passed away. And the sea is no longer. And I saw the holy city, New Jerusalem, coming down out of heaven from God prepared as a bride adorned for her man. And I heard a great voice out of heaven saying, 'Behold! The tabernacle of God is in the midst of men and he will abide with them and they shall be His people and He shall be their God and God Himself shall be with them.' And God shall wipe away every tear from their eyes and death shall be no more and neither shall there be any mourning or crying or pain because the first things have passed away." (Revelation 21.1-5)